THE STILLBORN LOVER

Timothy Findley
The Stillborn Lover

Harper*Perennial*Canada

For Martha Henry
and William Hutt

www.harpercanada.com

HarperCollins books may be purchased for
educational, business, or sales promotional use.
For information please write:
Special Markets Department
HarperCollins Canada
2 Bloor Street East, 20th Floor
Toronto, Ontario M4W 1A8

First published by Blizzard Publishing Inc. 1993
First HarperPerennial Canada edition 2003

National Library of Canada Cataloguing in
Publication

Findley, Timothy, 1930–2002
The stillborn lover / Timothy Findley.

ISBN 0-00-639255-5

I. Title.

PS8511.I38S75 2003   C812'.54   C2002-904696-3
PR9199.3.F52S75 2003

RRD 9 8 7 6 5 4 3

Printed and bound in the United States
Set in Palatino

The Stillborn Lover was co-produced by The Grand Theatre, London, Ontario, and the National Arts Centre, Ottawa, Ontario, and premièred by The Grand Theatre on March 26, 1993, with the following cast:

HARRY	William Hutt
MARIAN	Martha Henry
MICHAEL	Donald Davis
JULIET	Patricia Collins
DIANA	Kate Trotter
JACKMAN	Hardee T. Lineham
MAHAVOLITCH	Michael McManus

Directed by Peter Moss
Set and costumes designed by Astrid Janson
Lighting designed by Paul Mathiesen
Original music by Boko Suzuki
Sound designed by Jim Neil
Stage Manager: Brian Scott
Assistant Stage Manager: Nancy Dryden

The Stillborn Lover opened at the National Arts Centre on April 29, 1993.

Characters

HARRY: Harry Raymond, Canadian Ambassador to
   Moscow; mid- to late-sixties

MARIAN: Marian Raymond, his wife; late fifties.

DIANA: Diana Marsden, their daughter; a recently
   divorced lawyer, mid-twenties.

MICHAEL: Michael Riordon, Canada's Minister of External Affairs, touted as the next party leader; mid- to late-
   sixties.

JULIET: Juliet Riordon, his wife; late fifties, early sixties.

JACKMAN: Superintendent, RCMP B-Operations; forties.

MAHAVOLITCH: Corporal, RCMP, his junior partner; late
   twenties.

Set

Nominally, the setting is a safe house overlooking the
Ottawa River at Rockcliffe. As the play unfolds, settings in
other locations are evoked—a garden in Nagasaki, a courtyard and a bedroom in Cairo, a breakfast room and an
antechamber in the Riordon house.

The set itself is a series of platforms, some of them angled,
all of varying heights, and one of them, downstage, jutting
out "dangerously" over the orchestra. Steps and walkways
join the platforms.

Some wicker furniture, a garden bench, a bed, some louvered shutters, a great swatch of mosquito netting will be
wanted. The rest is light and, perhaps, projected silhou-
ettes—a palm tree, a window, a tiled roof, etc.

Music is provided by guitar, piano, and flute.

The action of the play takes place in 1972 and earlier, to
the 1940s.

Prelude

(*The house is perched on a steep ravine that drops down to a river. The house appears to float in space—insubstantial, tenuous—adrift amongst autumn leaves that fade toward distant hills.*
MUSIC: *flute, with a Japanese flavour, accompanies and supports the following, which may, as in the original production, be a spoken voice-over.*)

MARIAN: In Japan, there is an ancient game called Go. Its ritual moves are played on a squared-off board. Every move is made with a round, smooth stone. Once the stones have been set in place, they cannot be withdrawn. Their positions are locked, irrevocable. Like the moves and gestures we make with our lives.

(*The LIGHTS fade. The MUSIC concludes on a single, drifting note.*)

Act One

SCENE ONE

(*Autumn. Late afternoon. On one of the platforms, wicker furniture is piled beneath dust cloths. Downstage, there is a stone bench. The stage is empty of people. Far off, a dog barks. Silence.*)

JULIET: (*Off.*) How lovely! I'd forgotten.

DIANA: (*Off.*) I can't believe you'd give it up . . .

JULIET: (*Off.*) I can't believe it either.

DIANA: (*Off.*) Do we have to go in through the house? Can't we go this way?

MICHAEL: (*Off.*) I don't see why not.

(DIANA *enters the garden. She wears a tailored overcoat and a dark beret with a diamond pin on it.*)

DIANA: Oh . . . Wonderful.

(MICHAEL *enters—pausing to let the others pass before him.*)

MICHAEL: You care for that, Diana?

DIANA: Yes. Oh, yes. Father? Do come . . . The view!

(JULIET *enters—followed by* HARRY. *All are wearing light overcoats—autumn clothing.*)

JULIET: There you go, Harry. Diana wants to show you the river.

(HARRY *crosses to* DIANA. JULIET *lets him pass, hanging back near* MICHAEL.)

DIANA: Don't look till you get here, Father. Don't. There. How about that!

HARRY: Yes . . .

DIANA: Nothing anywhere beats the view up that river. Not in October.

JULIET: (*Taking* MICHAEL'*s arm.*) We were so happy here. Weren't we, Mike—all those years ago. Of all the houses everywhere in our lives, we were never better off than here.

MICHAEL: True enough. I guess . . .

(MAHAVOLITCH *and* JACKMAN *enter. Both wear raincoats and both carry hand luggage—* MAHAVOLITCH *a good deal more than* JACKMAN.)

I'm afraid you'll have to take that in the other way.

MAHAVOLITCH: Yessir.

(MAHAVOLITCH *and* JACKMAN *prepare to exit.*)

MICHAEL: Once you're inside, you might unlock that door. (*Referring to the sunroom, where furniture is piled.*) Where's Mrs. Raymond?

JACKMAN: Can't say, Minister. Thought she'd come around with you and Ambassador Raymond.

MICHAEL: No. No. (*He looks at* RAYMOND.) Harry?

HARRY: Yes, Mike . . . (*Slight pause.*) What is it?

JULIET: Where's Marian?

HARRY: I don't know. Didn't she . . . ?

DIANA: (*Breaking away, calling.*) Mother . . . ?

MICHAEL: She can't have gone far . . .

(MAHAVOLITCH *and* JACKMAN *start to set down the luggage.*)

No. Get them into the house. We'll find Mrs. Raymond.

MAHAVOLITCH: Yes, Minister.

(*They exit—with luggage—*JACKMAN *again making sure that* MAHAVOLITCH *carries most of it.* MICHAEL *watches* HARRY, *who has not moved from his place.*)

HARRY: (*Finally.*) I don't understand. Marian was definitely with us.

DIANA: (*Calling.*) Mother . . . ? (*She exits.*)

HARRY: . . . I'm sure of it.

JULIET: Not to worry.

HARRY: Marian?

JULIET: No. Let me . . . Diana and I will find her. (*She starts to exit.*)

HARRY: Thank you, Juliet. (*Pause.*) I'm sorry, Mike.

MICHAEL: She'll turn up. (*He looks around the garden.*) You know, it's quite true. I guess we were happier here in this house than anywhere else we've ever lived . . . me and Juliet. And we've certainly had our share of cities. Santiago, Moscow, London . . .

(MAHAVOLITCH *and* JACKMAN *appear in the sunroom and unlock the doors—after which they begin to*

arrange the furniture, taking off the dust sheets, etc.
MICHAEL *looks at the river.*)

Imagine, after all that—to say that you were happiest in Ottawa, of all places. But, oh dear God . . . those hills—that river . . . and, of course, our children were born here.

HARRY: Yes.

MICHAEL: Diana was born . . . Where was it? Japan?

HARRY: That's right.

MICHAEL: Nagasaki?

HARRY: Yes.

MICHAEL: Wonderful, isn't it—the useless information a person stores.

HARRY: Next thing you know, you'll remember where you were born.

MICHAEL: I'm sorry. That was completely thoughtless.

HARRY: Yes, it was. But I forgive you . . . (*He smiles.*)

MICHAEL: (*Smiling.*) Thank you.

DIANA and JULIET: (*Off, variously.*) Mother . . . ?
Marian . . . ?

MICHAEL: (*Pause.*) Have you talked with her . . . with
Marian . . . about why you might be here?

HARRY: How could I do that? I don't know why we're
here. (*Pause.*) All we were told was: I've been called
home on "special duty."

MICHAEL: Yes. Well.

HARRY: I guess we all know what that means.

MICHAEL: (*Making light of it.*) Do we, now.

HARRY: Oh, for Christ's sake, Mike. Being called home on
"special duty" is just a polite way of saying there's
going to be an investigation. What I don't know is why.

(*Off-stage, the dog barks again in the distance.*)

Why are we here, Mike? And at whose instigation?

(MICHAEL *does not answer.*)

Was it yours?

MICHAEL: I'm only a servant, Harry. Just a servant—like
you.

HARRY: Like hell you are. You're bloody Minister of External Affairs.

MICHAEL: Yes. But in matters like·these, the bloody Minister of External Affairs is just a servant. We will talk about it tomorrow.

HARRY: But...

MICHAEL: *Tomorrow.* (*Beat.*) Today, rest. That's a hell of a journey you've just made. Moscow to here—non-stop.

JULIET and DIANA: (*Off, variously.*) Marian...? Mother...?

HARRY: Yes. I'm tired.

JULIET: (*Off.*) Yoo-hoo! Marian...?

MICHAEL: What about this, Harry? Disappearing like this...

HARRY: Marian? It's part of her condition.

MICHAEL: Ah...

HARRY: Yes, Alzheimer's. The disease with no design. Plays havoc with the memory. Like this—being lost. In Moscow, she would disappear for hours. It was nerve-wracking. Once, she came back to the Embassy with blood on her dress. "Where have you been?" "I don't know." "Why is there blood?" "I don't know." The good thing is—so far—she's always managed to find her way home.

MICHAEL: Thank god for that.

HARRY: (*Lightly.*) We're coping, of course. Oh, yes—sometimes we don't even know when she's in the disease. I don't know—she doesn't. And there's no medication. But we're coping. We're coping.

MICHAEL: I'm sorry, Harry. I am. Look, you must have an A-1 case of jet lag. Let's just . . . celebrate the fact you're here. Shall we? (*He indicates the sunroom.*) Why don't you and I find a drink?

(*They go to the steps,* HARRY *hanging back.*)

She'll turn up. They'll find her.

(MICHAEL *and* HARRY *join* MAHAVOLITCH *and* JACKMAN *in the sunroom.* MICHAEL *says a few words to them and then leads* HARRY *up the stairway into the body of the house.*)

SCENE TWO

(MUSIC: *a chord that lingers.*)

DIANA and JULIET: (*Off, variously.*) Mother . . . ?
   Marian . . . ?

(MUSIC: *a severed chord.*)

Marian . . . ? Mother . . . ?

(MARIAN *enters. She carries an open umbrella and a bou-
quet of flowers wrapped in paper. She looks at the garden
around her and then she stares at the river.*
MUSIC: *a resolving chord.*
MARIAN *closes her eyes and wavers.* DIANA *enters.*)

DIANA: Mother . . .

MARIAN: Where have you been, Diana? I've been looking
   for you everywhere.

DIANA: (*Laughing.*) I've been looking for you!

MARIAN: Are you cold? I thought I heard Juliet.

DIANA: You did. She's . . . Mother, you can put the
   umbrella down. It's not raining. (DIANA *does this for
   her.*) And do you want me to hold the flowers?

(*She takes them.*)

MARIAN: Just remember they're mine.

(*She sits on the garden bench, placing umbrella beneath it.*)

All the leaves are turning red. Winter's coming. Not my favourite. Maybe the reason they've brought us back is to give your father a posting in the sun. You think? Perhaps . . . ?

DIANA: I can't answer that. Everything happened so quickly. I got a phone call: "Your parents are arriving. Come to Uplands!" That's really all I know.

MARIAN: (*Merely saying it.*) Liar . . .

DIANA: It's true, Mother. I can't tell you anything . . .

(*Still at some distance, the dog barks.* MARIAN *waves her hand for silence.* DIANA *listens.*)

It's only some dog. Down by the river. (*Beat.*) All I know is, you're here—and I'm glad you're here.

MARIAN: Is he lost, that dog? Look—there's Juliet.

(JULIET *enters.*)

Somebody's lost their dog. Is it yours? Were you looking? Is that where you've been all this time? Have you seen the house? Whose is it? Maybe it's their dog. Whoever lives here . . .

DIANA: I don't really think so, Mother. The house has been empty for a long time. This is where you're going to be staying—you and Father—until we know what's going to happen next.

MARIAN: I hope whatever happens next is somewhere in the sun. Anywhere but . . . *what's-its-face* . . .

DIANA: Australia, maybe. You haven't had Australia.

MARIAN: (*Ignoring* DIANA.) Did you ever have to suffer the wonders of *what's-its-face*, Juliet?

JULIET: *What's-it* . . . where?

(*She looks at* DIANA.)

DIANA: Moscow.

MARIAN: What makes you so certain I mean Moscow? (*Turning.*) Have you, Juliet?

JULIET: What?

MARIAN: Been there?

JULIET: Where?

MARIAN: *Moscow.*

JULIET: Yes. That was our last posting . . .

MARIAN: Muscovites are pigs . . .

JULIET: . . . before Mike became Minister.

MARIAN: Swine.

JULIET: Yes—well . . . We rather enjoyed it there. I think it's one of the most beautiful embassies we have.

MARIAN: We haven't been to India. Maybe they'll give us India. You think?

DIANA: Maybe there won't be a posting at all. Maybe they'll let you rest for a while.

MARIAN: Rest? Not here, pray God.

DIANA: I think Father looks tired. Don't you, Juliet?

MARIAN: We will not rest here. (*She listens.*) Oh, that poor dog . . .

JULIET: Whether you end up in India or Timbuktu isn't something for us to decide. That's what I've always loved most about External . . . someone else makes all your decisions. The only thing you have to do is catch the right plane. (*To* D I A N A.) Let me take those . . . (*She takes the flowers; speaks quietly.*) Don't you think we should get her inside?

(M A R I A N *suddenly walks down stage.* M I C H A E L *comes into the sunroom carrying a drink and an 8 × 10 government issue envelope with seals. He has removed his topcoat.* M A H A V O L I T C H *and* J A C K M A N *have finished setting the furniture in place. Whatever conversation they have with* M I C H A E L *is not heard—but their talk is obviously about the Raymonds—* H A R R Y, *somewhere in the house, and* M A R I A N, *in the garden. Also about the contents of the envelope, which* M I C H A E L *passes to* J A C K M A N.)

M A R I A N: I heard that. I don't want to go inside. You know—I swear I've been in this garden before.

J U L I E T: You have.

M A R I A N: That view. The river . . .

(M A R I A N *moves onto the jutting platform.*)

J U L I E T: Mike and I lived here after the war. You came to visit us when Diana was still a baby. You'd just returned from Japan.

M A R I A N: There was a swing over there . . .

JULIET: That's right . . .

MARIAN: Hanging from that tree . . .

JULIET: That's right . . .

DIANA: What tree?

MARIAN: And I used to swing . . . way out over the edge.

DIANA: What tree? Where?

JULIET: We cut it down.

MARIAN: And the view was . . .

DIANA: Isn't that funny . . .

MARIAN: (*At the edge.*) . . . electrifying . . .

(HARRY, *minus topcoat, appears on one of the upper plat-forms. He looks down into the garden.*)

DIANA: I don't remember any tree . . .

MARIAN: Wonderful! You could swing right into the sky.

DIANA: . . . why did you cut it down?

JULIET: It was old, I guess. I don't remember.

MARIAN: Dangerous and marvelous! I used to have
dreams about letting go. Just letting go and sailing out
over that ravine . . . *kerplop!*

(DIANA *laughs.*)

With you in my lap.

DIANA: Me?

MARIAN: Yes. Baby Diana—in her swaddling clothes.

DIANA: But only in your dreams . . .

MARIAN: Don't be afraid. I never let go of you. Not for an
instant.

DIANA: Well—thank you. Did we . . . *land?*

MARIAN: But, of course.

DIANA: In my dreams—when I'm falling, I never land.

MARIAN: Well—in my dreams, I do.

JULIET: *Kerplop . . .*

(DIANA *shoots* JULIET *a look.* JULIET *shrugs and
smiles.* HARRY *moves away from window.*)

DIANA: (*To* MARIAN.) Are we destroyed?

MARIAN: Destroyed.

DIANA: When we land . . . are we killed?

MARIAN: Well, of course we are. You don't think you could fall that distance and not be killed, do you?

DIANA: No. But in dreams, things are different . . .

MARIAN: Tell her, Juliet . . . how we used to sail out over that ravine. She doesn't believe me.

JULIET: All I remember is the tree . . .

MARIAN: (*Dispassionately.*) Liar.

(HARRY *exits.*)

JULIET: And the swing, of course. I remember the swing.

(MICHAEL *comes to the edge of the sunroom.*)

MICHAEL: How would you ladies like to come in and have a drink . . . take a look around?

(MAHAVOLITCH *and* JACKMAN *exit.*)

JULIET: Good idea. It's getting cold. (*She turns.*) I'm going
   to put these in water.

(JULIET *makes for the steps, but* MARIAN *and* DIANA
hang back.)

Is the inside still as lovely as it was?

MICHAEL: A little barren perhaps. But we can rectify all that.

(JULIET *exits. The dog barks in the ravine.*)

MARIAN: Maybe he's found our shattered bones, Diana—
   yours and mine—hidden all these years beneath the
   leaves.

(MARIAN *turns and heads for the sunroom.* DIANA
remains down stage. HARRY *enters the sunroom carrying a
tray with bottles and glasses on it.*)

HARRY: One thing about a safe house, Mike—wherever
   they are, whatever their purpose—they always have
   the best liquor.

MICHAEL: Yes. And plenty of it.

(MARIAN *has been on the instant of entering the sunroom,
but she stops in her tracks.*)

MARIAN: Safe house? Did Harry say *safe house*?

(*No one answers.*
Hold. The LIGHTS *fade—except on* DIANA*, down stage.*)

SCENE THREE

(DIANA *crosses to the jutting edge and stares down into the*
ravine. JACKMAN *comes into the garden from the side of*
the house. He watches her for a moment.)

JACKMAN: Steep, isn't it.

DIANA: Yes.

JACKMAN: Sometimes—not very often—you get the smell
of sulphur from the other side of the river. The pulp
mills.

DIANA: Yes.

JACKMAN: Otherwise, beautiful. The perfect location.

DIANA: What for?

JACKMAN: Sorry?

DIANA: Perfect location for what?

JACKMAN: Well—the view, of course.

DIANA: Of the river—or my parents? You're with the
    RCMP, aren't you.

JACKMAN: You've got it, Miss Raymond.

DIANA: (*Moving into the garden.*) I'm not Miss Raymond.

JACKMAN: Well . . .

DIANA: My name is Marsden. Diana Marsden. And
    what's your name?

JACKMAN: Jackman.

DIANA: Is that it? Just Jackman?

JACKMAN: Superintendent Jackman, RCMP.

DIANA: Yes—I was forgetting. You people never do have
    first names, do you.

JACKMAN: Danny . . .

DIANA: It doesn't really suit you, does it: *Danny* . . .

JACKMAN: Well—it's *Daniel*, to be right about it. But I've
    had Danny all my life. What name might you find more
    suitable, Mrs. Marsden?

DIANA: Oh—I don't know. Clint, or something. Burt.

JACKMAN: I see. So your impression of me is just about the same as my impression of you: *wrong*.

DIANA: What do you mean by that?

JACKMAN: That I *did* know your name was Marsden . . . if it matters. But you've been divorced and I thought you must've reverted. Most women do, these days. Revert to their maiden name.

DIANA: I'm not, and never was a maiden, Superintendent.

JACKMAN: Well. Score one for you.

DIANA: So . . . what else *don't* you know about me?

JACKMAN: Not much, I guess. Maybe what colour your underwear is. I *do* know how many husbands you've had and why you divorced them. What books you read. What pills you take—and why. The fact that you're a lawyer. I could name all your clients, if you want me to . . .

DIANA: No thank you.

JACKMAN: I know how many cases you've won—how many you've lost—how much money you make. What sort of clients you prefer . . .

DIANA: You're very thorough.

JACKMAN: It's my job, Mrs. Marsden. There's more, if you want to hear it.

DIANA: No.

JACKMAN: I wouldn't want you to think your father and mother were in careless hands.

DIANA: Are they in protective custody? Surely you can tell me that. Are they in danger?

JACKMAN: There's all kinds of danger, Mrs. Marsden. Isn't there.

(*He smiles.* DIANA *stares at him for a moment — and then she crosses to the steps. In the sunroom, muted voices are raised.*)

DIANA: Are you coming in, Superintendent?

JACKMAN: Not just yet.

DIANA: I wish I could say it had been a pleasure talking to you.

JACKMAN: No you don't, ma'am. But I'll accept the sentiment.

(DIANA *goes up the steps and into the sunroom. There is another burst of voices.* MARIAN *hurries to her and takes her arm as if* DIANA*'s presence will make everything all right.* JACKMAN *goes to the edge and looks into the ravine. Pause. The dog barks.* JACKMAN *brightens. He nods—as if in response to a signal from below. Then he waves. The* LIGHTS *dim.)*

SCENE FOUR

(The sunroom. MARIAN *removes her outer coat and puts it first over one chair and then another. She then becomes pre-occupied with a spot on her collar—her back to the audience.)*

HARRY: Good for you, Diana. I was beginning to think you'd deserted us. Have a drink.

DIANA: Thank you, Father. Is Mother . . . ?

HARRY: (*Ignoring her question.*) We were just discussing futures.

DIANA: Futures—yes. Exciting—for some. (*To* MICHAEL.) You're to be the next PM, I understand.

MICHAEL: Nothing is certain.

DIANA: How could they resist you, Michael. I think it's splendid. Your health.

MICHAEL: Thank you, Diana.

HARRY: When does it happen?

MICHAEL: The convention is in four weeks. Slightly less.

HARRY: And you're a shoo-in?

MICHAEL: So they tell me.

HARRY: I'm out of touch.

MICHAEL: Not really. The momentum is fairly recent. Two months ago, we thought he was going to get better.

HARRY: The Prime Minister.

MICHAEL: Yes. It *is* a cancer. Inoperable. Nothing's being said. Just that he wants to spend more time with his family. The usual—write his memoirs—enjoy the sunset.

HARRY: He's been Prime Minister eight years.

MICHAEL: Yes. And it's been a good eight years. Good for him—good for the country—and very good for the Party.

(JULIET *enters with the flowers in a vase.*)

HARRY: How old is he now?

JULIET: Who?

MICHAEL: The PM.

MARIAN: (*Not turning.*) Seventy-one.

(*Everyone looks at her. She is unaware of it, concentrating on the spot.*)

JULIET: (*Showing the flowers.*) Aren't they beautiful.

MARIAN: Where did you get those?

JULIET: Why, I . . .

MARIAN: They're mine.

JULIET: Of course they are, dear. I gave them to you when you got off the plane. Remember? I was just putting them in water.

(*She sets the flowers on a table.*)

MARIAN: Everyone keeps taking everything. Where's my umbrella?

DIANA: I thought you had it, Mother.

MARIAN: You had it.

DIANA: No. I folded it up and gave it back to you, in the garden.

MARIAN: When?

JULIET: I wouldn't worry about your umbrella, dear. It hasn't rained here in days.

MARIAN: Do you call everyone "dear," Juliet? Or just people you don't like?

JULIET: (*Getting a drink.*) My goodness. We are cranky, aren't we . . .

MARIAN: I heard that. First I'm "dear"—and then I'm "we." People have names, Juliet.

JULIET: Yes, Marian.

MARIAN: I also happen not to be crazy.

JULIET: No one said you were.

MARIAN: You said cranky. Cranky means crazy.

DIANA: (*Laughing.*) Oh—Mother—for heaven's sake!

MARIAN: It's German, *Krankenhaus*. That's the crazy-
house. The loony bin.

(HARRY *walks away. He cannot bear this.* MICHAEL
watches him.)

JULIET: (*To* MICHAEL.) Should we leave? (*She smiles.*)
Let these people get some rest . . . ?

HARRY: No. Please. Finish your drinks.

(MAHAVOLITCH *and* JACKMAN *enter the garden.*
JACKMAN *sits on the bench, facing the audience.*
MAHAVOLITCH *swings an imaginary golf club.*)

MAHAVOLITCH: Whammo!

JACKMAN: You missed.

(MAHAVOLITCH *sits on the bench facing the sunroom.*)

JULIET: Well! The election process begins. Tomorrow
night, cocktails and a dinner party. Sixty people. Under
our own roof! Can you believe it? I thought we'd done
all that in our embassy days. But . . . (*She waves her
hands.*) here we go again. Of course, it's different when
you have a staff—the way you do when you're abroad.
Still—I've got help coming in. Call themselves The
Commissariats. Sounds like a Russian rock band, to

me. They're kids. Students. They never know where anything is. They offer to bring their own stuff but I said yes to that, once, and the silly twits turned up with paper plates. And plastic champagne glasses. I said: "We aren't serving champagne." One of the girls made a face and said: "I thought this was going to be a class act." It's because we're in North America, of course. You wouldn't catch a Brit with a paper plate! Not in ten million . . . Well, I did once. But it was the American Embassy. A garden party. There's some excuse for that. If you're celebrating Walt Disney's birthday—and all the guests are two.

DIANA: My goodness, Juliet. Sixty. Where will you seat them all?

JULIET: Garden tables.

DIANA: In this weather?

JULIET: No, no, Diana. Indoors. But at garden tables. I saw it in a magazine. I thought it was so clever. Garden furniture is so sturdy. Nice big round tables—lovely little chairs. Everything white . . .

MICHAEL: Classy. (*He winks at* HARRY.)

JULIET: Yes. Well. Ingenuity. That's what counts. I dread it, of course. The dear PM with his dire disease will be there. He's being wonderful to Mike—absolutely wonderful.

Shows up—even in pain—and waves the flag. This thing tomorrow is a mix of the converted and the unconverted. What Michael calls the Party-*pros* and the Party-*poopers*.

MARIAN: The *patsies* and the *shit-disturbers*.

JULIET: That's right, Marian. Call a spade a spade. (*Beat.*) Of course, it's different, now that we're in politics. The rules are different. As the ambassador's wife, I used to memorize people's faces. Now, as the candidate's wife, I memorize their shoes. In politics, every time you turn around, there's a whole new set of toes not to step on. Yes, Michael?

(MICHAEL *waves his hand.*)

And the obfuscation! The manipulation! The first thing I learned when we got back to Ottawa was that I didn't have to smile any more when I told a lie. Abroad, as the ambassador's wife, I used to think of cocktail parties as *discretion-sessions*. Here, we have *deception-receptions*. But then, I'm the one who use to think that gerrymandering meant *taking care of the Germans* . . .

MICHAEL: It does—in Germany.

JULIET: I think we'd better leave.

MICHAEL: Yes.

MARIAN: This event, Juliet—what is it, tomorrow?

JULIET: A dinner party.

MARIAN: Are we invited?

(*No one knows what to say.*)

DIANA: You're having dinner with me, tomorrow,
Mother. Good-bye, Juliet. Michael.

JULIET: Good-bye, all.

MICHAEL: (*Aside.*) Walk me to the front door, Harry.
You're right. We need to have a word.

HARRY: Certainly.

MICHAEL: You go on ahead, Juliet. I'll be with you in a
moment.

(*The* LIGHTS *fade slightly in the sunroom as* HARRY
leads MICHAEL *and* JULIET *off.* MARIAN *stands and
stares out the window.* DIANA *watches her.*)

MAHAVOLITCH: (*Turns to face the audience.*) So. When do
we begin?

JACKMAN: We already have.

MAHAVOLITCH: Oh? How?

JACKMAN: Just go on sitting here. It makes them nervous.

(JULIET *appears on one of the walkways between plat-forms. She is putting on her gloves in obvious distress.*)

JULIET: Shit. (*She looks back.*)

(MICHAEL *enters behind her.*)

You didn't have to make me do that.

MICHAEL: Do what?

JULIET: Prattle.

MICHAEL: It's your great, good talent, Juliet. Be grateful.

JULIET: But they're our friends.

MICHAEL: Precisely.

JULIET: You don't prattle at friends, Mike.

MICHAEL: You do when they're in trouble.

JULIET: Oh, god. That poor woman. (*She takes his arm.*)
I've never seen a woman so obviously distressed. She
nearly bit my head off.

MICHAEL: Yes.

JULIET: She doesn't know yet, does she. Why they're here.

MICHAEL: No. I've only just told Harry. Now—he will tell her. And Diana.

JULIET: What? What will he tell them?

(MICHAEL *stops, and looks at her.*)

MICHAEL: Harry and Marian are here, Juliet. They've come home. That's all I can tell you.

(MICHAEL *exits.* JULIET *looks back at the sunroom and at* MARIAN. *Then she exits.*)

MARIAN: There are two men out there.

DIANA: Yes.

MARIAN: I want to go home.

DIANA: We are home, Mother.

(*The* LIGHTS *fade altogether on the two women.*)

MAHAVOLITCH: Somebody left their umbrella behind.

(*He has found the umbrella under the bench. Now, he raises it. They sit for a moment. Then* JACKMAN *puts his hand out, palm up.*)

JACKMAN: You're right. It's raining.

(MAHAVOLITCH *does the same.*)

MAHAVOLITCH: No, it's not.

JACKMAN: Yes, it is.

MAHAVOLITCH: No, it's not.

(JACKMAN *rises.*)

JACKMAN: Yes. It is, Corporal Mahavolitch.

(*Takes umbrella and holds it over himself.*)

It is pouring.

(MAHAVOLITCH *slowly rises.*)

Come on.

(*As they exit,* MAHAVOLITCH *looks at the sky, shrugs, and turns his collar up.*
MUSIC: *segue.*)

SCENE FIVE

(*Sunroom.* MARIAN *stands where she was, staring at the garden.* DIANA *is near the vase of flowers.* HARRY *enters.* MICHAEL *has now told him why he has been brought home. He is agitated, hyperactive. He crosses to the table where bottles and glasses and ice await him. He prepares a drink for each of them.*)

DIANA: (*To* HARRY.) So. Now what?

HARRY: Now, we wait.

DIANA: For what?

HARRY: To hear what they have to say. In the morning.

DIANA: You don't know what they're going to say?

HARRY: (*Lying.*) No. Not precisely.

DIANA: What about Mother?

HARRY: Your mother will be fine. She needs to rest.

DIANA: (*Accepting a drink.*) Look at her. So still. I had no idea she was so badly off. It must be very hard on you, Father.

HARRY: Yes. But worse, of course, for her.

(HARRY *approaches* MARIAN *with her drink. She does not move or look at him.*)

Marian?

MARIAN: Why have they brought us here, Harry?

HARRY: I don't know, yet. They haven't told me.

MARIAN: Liar.

(*She looks at him. He offers her the drink. She ignores it.*)

You think I don't know what a safe house is for?

(*She takes cigarettes from her handbag—gets one out and looks for her lighter.*)

I do remember *some* things, you know. It's not *all* gone, up here. I do remember *some* things . . .

(*She cannot find her lighter.*)

HARRY: Of course you do.

MARIAN: Don't you patronize me, you bastard. Why are they hiding us? Why are we being hidden, Harry? They found you out, didn't they? How? What have you done?

(DIANA *is watching* HARRY.)

HARRY: Nothing.

MARIAN: We're not in hiding for "nothing," Harry.

HARRY: Don't stare at me, Diana. Light your mother's cigarette.

(HARRY *puts* MARIAN*'s drink on a nearby table and goes back to the drinks table.* DIANA *lights* MARIAN*'s cigarette.* MARIAN *looks at* DIANA *through her smoke.*)

MARIAN: Do you call that thing a hat?

DIANA: I call it a beret.

MARIAN: Does that pin thing belong to me?

DIANA: No, Mother. It's mine.

MARIAN: (*Picking up her drink.*) I never wear hats. I hate them. The only reason people wear hats is because they have something to hide. Are you going bald?

DIANA: No, Mother.

(MARIAN *leans in close to* DIANA *and whispers.*)

MARIAN: Do you know why we're here?

DIANA: No.

MARIAN: It's a posting. They're going to give us another posting.

(HARRY *coughs.*)

Why can't we go to Mexico? I want to go to Mexico. Hot white sand. Cool white houses. In Cairo . . . In Cairo we had red tile floors and ceiling fans. Balconies. I sat in the sun for days on end. Your father loved it there . . . Didn't you, Harry—love it there in Cairo.

HARRY: Yes.

MARIAN: Diana says they're giving us Mexico.

(HARRY *glances at* DIANA. DIANA *shakes her head.*)

Won't that be wonderful? Just to get out of the cold. That's all I want.

HARRY: We've done Mexico, Marian. Years ago.

MARIAN: Have we?

HARRY: Yes. (*Beat.*) They'll tell you this in the morning, anyhow. I might as well tell you now.

MARIAN: What? Another lie?

HARRY: No. Not a lie. (*Beat.*) Mike just told me. (*Beat.*)

(MAHAVOLITCH *appears on an upper level. He puts a suitcase on the floor. He begins to undress. There is a straight-back chair for him to lay clothing on.*)

There's been a killing. In Moscow. A young man. They found the body in a hotel room.

DIANA: So?

HARRY: Questions are being asked.

DIANA: (*Coming down the stairs.*) Why? Was he a Canadian? One of your staff?

HARRY: No.

DIANA: Then—what's it got to do with you? (*Beat.*) Did you know him? Did Mother know him? What's the connection?

HARRY: He was murdered . . .

(MAHAVOLITCH *by now is shirtless.*)

DIANA: But what's that got to do with you and Mother being returned to Canada?

MARIAN: It was him, wasn't it Harry.

(*She sits.* MAHAVOLITCH *undoes his belt and zipper.*)

HARRY: Yes.

DIANA: Who?

MARIAN: Mischa . . .

(MAHAVOLITCH *kicks off his loafers.*)

DIANA: Daddy?

(MAHAVOLITCH *"freezes." The stair-door opens.* JACKMAN *enters the sunroom.*)

JACKMAN: Excuse me?

HARRY: I said we wanted to be alone!

JACKMAN: Sorry. We found this umbrella.

(*He leaves it and exits.*)

MARIAN: Bang.

HARRY: What?

MARIAN: *Bang!* The umbrella just exploded.

DIANA: Tell me who he was. The young man—the dead man.

(MAHAVOLITCH *removes his trousers.*)

Who *was* he? Mother knew his name.

(HARRY *walks away.*)

MARIAN: He was a friend. Of mine. (*Beat.*) Of your
father's.

DIANA: Murdered?

HARRY: Yes.

DIANA: My god.

HARRY: Indeed.

(DIANA *looks at* MARIAN. *Suddenly,* DIANA *sits
down. She closes her eyes. When she opens them, she stares at*
HARRY *with her hand across her mouth.*)

We know nothing, Diana. Nothing.

MARIAN: (*Quietly.*) Liar.

(*The* LIGHTS *fade in the sunroom.*)

SCENE SIX

(MAHAVOLITCH, *now in his shorts, crouches by his suitcase. He opens it and removes his service revolver. Then he stands up and straps it on with a shoulder holster. He crosses to an imaginary mirror, his back to the audience. Watching himself, he removes his shorts and stands there—contented.* MUSIC: *a conclusion.* LIGHTS *fade on upper platform.*)

SCENE SEVEN

(*Walkway. Evening.* DIANA *alone. Her beret is off, her coat around her shoulders. In the sunroom,* MARIAN *rises.*)

MARIAN: Why didn't you tell me? (*She begins to exit.*) Why didn't you tell me?

HARRY: (*Following her.*) How could I tell you? I didn't know.

(*Both exit.*)

MARIAN: (*Off.*) Oh, god. Dead.

(*There is the* SOUND *of a door closing.* DIANA *sighs.* JACKMAN *enters—on a different level or platform.*)

JACKMAN: A bit cool to be standing about.

DIANA: I don't mind. Where's your friend?

JACKMAN: Gone running. He's a health nut.

DIANA: Ah—yes.

JACKMAN: Not my style. Never was. Give me an armchair every time. May I join you?

DIANA: You already have.

JACKMAN: (*With humour.*) Is it me you don't like? Or just men?

DIANA: You.

(JACKMAN *moves to her vicinity.*)

And you? Is it me you like? Or just women?

JACKMAN: Women.

DIANA: Thank heaven for that.

JACKMAN: Pleasant evening—in spite of the cool.

DIANA: I was counting stars.

JACKMAN: (*Looking.*) There only is one.

DIANA: That's right. One.

JACKMAN: When you get to *two*, let me know.

DIANA: Two now—if the moon is a star.

JACKMAN: No. The moon is just the moon, ma'am. (*Pause.*) It was decent of you to stay on. They'll be needing you.

DIANA: I was told to stay on.

JACKMAN: Oh—really?

DIANA: Yes. By the Minister. Don't play pussyfoot with me, Superintendent. Why don't you ask your first question?

JACKMAN: You know why they're here? Why they've been brought back?

DIANA: There's a dead man.

JACKMAN: That's right. A young Russian.

DIANA: I gather my parents knew him.

JACKMAN: Yes. They did.

DIANA: This young man, so I gather, was murdered. He

was a friend of my mother's. Has my father been accused of this?

JACKMAN: Not yet.

DIANA: But he's a suspect.

JACKMAN: You've got it.

DIANA: But that's preposterous. What makes you think my father could commit a murder?

JACKMAN: What makes you think he couldn't?

DIANA: Oh, *please!*

(*She moves away from him.*)

JACKMAN: (*Amused.*) That doesn't sound much like a lawyer's answer, Mrs. Marsden. Sounds more like a daughter's answer to me.

DIANA: I am a daughter. First and foremost—where my parents are concerned.

JACKMAN: Yes, ma'am.

DIANA: Must you call me "ma'am"?

JACKMAN: Yes, ma'am.

DIANA: You sound like a boy scout.

JACKMAN: There you are then. Me "boy scout." You "daughter." (*Beat.*) Any chance the policeman might get an answer from the lawyer?

DIANA: Not a chance in hell.

JACKMAN: You mean you aren't prepared to weigh the evidence?

DIANA: What evidence?

JACKMAN: Your father was *there*, Mrs. Marsden. Your father was there. The boy was not a stranger to him. What if . . . ?

DIANA: What if *what?*

JACKMAN: What if he killed him in self-defence? People do that, you know. Even good people.

DIANA: (*Coolly.*) Go on. Educate me.

JACKMAN: Put it this way, Mrs. Marsden: right now, you yourself are engaged in self-defence. It all depends how far the self extends, doesn't it . . .

(MARIAN *enters the garden—moonlit.*)

Some people think of their parents as being part of themselves. Yes? Parents think of their children that way. Husbands. Wives. Extensions of the self. So, when it comes to self-defence . . . You see my point, I trust.

(DIANA *has been watching* MARIAN.)

DIANA: (*Quietly.*) Yes. I see your point. (*Pause.*) My mother . . . My father . . . My parents, Mister Jackman, are (*Smiles.*) *uncommon folk.* Exceptional. They actually love one another. Can you imagine that? I regard them with a sense, I guess, of wonder—given what they've survived.

JACKMAN: You're telling me you love them.

DIANA: No. Respect—yes. Love? I'm not so sure.

JACKMAN: They been married long?

DIANA: Since the war. You know all this. You must've read the brief.

JACKMAN: It says you were born in Japan. Nagasaki.

DIANA: That's right. Nagasaki is where they went on their honeymoon, if you can believe it. That's what they were like. Idealists. Later, they went back, just so I could be born there. I think it was their gesture of atonement.

MARIAN: Harry?

JACKMAN: Your dad was in Japan with some sort of commission.

DIANA: Yes. (*Playing it.*) The Canadian Mission to the Supreme Commander for the Allied Powers for the Occupation and Control of Japan! SCAP!

MARIAN: Harry? Come out and see the moon.

DIANA: Mother was with them, too. As a cipher clerk.

(HARRY *enters the garden.*)

They were in their thirties, then. Young.

(MUSIC: *flute—a Japanese melody.*
HARRY *stands behind* MARIAN *with his hand on her shoulder. They look at the moon.*)

Do you ever try to imagine your parents, Superintendent . . . what they were like before you were born?

(LIGHTS *alter.*)

MARIAN: (*Younger.*) Tell me why you came to Japan.

HARRY: (*Younger.*) I was posted here. I had no choice.

MARIAN: Oh, come on. You could've said no.

HARRY: I didn't want to say *no*. I wanted to be here. I wanted to see what had been done. I didn't want to be "told," any more. We were being told so many lies.

MARIAN: You knew they were lies?

HARRY: Yes. Discretionary lies, of course.

MARIAN: About the bombs?

HARRY: Yes. (*Beat.*) You said *bombs*. Plural. That's interesting.

MARIAN: You think so?

HARRY: Yes.

MARIAN: It was deliberate. I say it to test the waters—see who I'm talking to. Most people let it pass. They don't even notice. What is it, now—not quite a year since they fell?

HARRY: Ten months, six days . . .

MARIAN: And ten months, three days. One—and then the other. Hiroshima. Nagasaki. The Japanese had already sued for peace before the first bomb fell. Did you know that?

HARRY: Perhaps you shouldn't be telling me this. Aren't things like that official secrets?

MARIAN: The war is over, Harry. I can tell you anything I like. About the war. Not about now, of course. Funny, isn't it? Here we are married—the cipher clerk and the junior diplomat—sworn to silence. What will we talk about in bed at night? Not our secrets. *Never*. Never our secrets. Only our lies. (*She laughs.*) Unless, of course, we talk in our sleep.

HARRY: The burden must have been unbearable, during the war. For you.

MARIAN: Yes. And no. It was just a job—if you didn't think about it. When you did think about it—what you knew—it was dreadful. Knowing when people would die. Hundreds of them—without warning . . . There were moments . . . There were moments when I wanted . . . wanted to stand in the street and shout out the truth. Which, of course, one never did. Sometimes, what you knew was wonderful. Like the suit for peace. It was July—last year: July, 1945—still not a year ago—good Lord! I was in England, then—a cipher clerk at Bletchley Park—part of a special liaison unit decoding intercepts sent on to us by the Americans. This particular intercept was of a message sent from Tokyo to the Japanese Embassy in Moscow. The Emperor had "brought his will to bear in favour of peace." Isn't that wonderful? The language of desperate diplomacy: *brought his will to bear in favour of peace.* I thought the war was over. Every minute of every day, I waited for the next intercept—the one that would say a surrender was in progress. It never came, of course. The message we got wasn't written in code. It was written in bombs. *Them.* One—and then the other. Hiroshima. Nagasaki. So much for peace.

HARRY: Yes.

MARIAN: There used to be a song about Nagasaki. Do you remember?

(*She sings.*)

Hot ginger and dynamite,
There's nothing but that at night—
Back in Nagasaki,
Where the fellows chew tobaccy,
And the women wicky-wacky
Woo!

(MARIAN *stops suddenly.*)

Dear God—I hate who we are. I hate what we've done.

HARRY: It's all right. It's all right.

MARIAN: Nothing will ever match the barbarity of that second bomb, Harry. Seventy-five thousand dead. To teach us all—a lesson.

HARRY: I love you, Marian.

MARIAN: Yes. And I love you. For all our sins.

(HARRY *and* MARIAN *exit.*)

DIANA: I was born of that moment. There in Nagasaki.

JACKMAN: (*Pause.*) Were your parents communists, Mrs. Marsden?

DIANA: That's right, Superintendent. Plotting the overthrow of everything we stand for. There isn't any hiding from your politics, is there. (*Leaving.*) Good night, Mister Jackman.

SCENE EIGHT

(*Morning. In the sunroom,* MAHAVOLITCH *is laying out files and papers taken from a briefcase. He wears a jogging suit with the* RCMP *logo on the breast-pocket.* HARRY *enters the garden. At a distance, the* SOUND *of Canada geese can be heard.* HARRY *stops to listen. Facing the audience, he sights them coming as if from the back of the auditorium. As the* SOUND *increases and the geese pass overhead,* HARRY *shades his eyes to see them.* MAHAVOLITCH *comes down to the sunroom widows from which he also watches the geese. When the geese are directly overhead,*

HARRY *raises his right arm in salutation. The* SOUND *of the geese is thrilling.* HARRY *turns all the way upstage as the geese pass over the roof of the house and the* SOUND *of them fades into the distance. Now, both men meet each other's gaze. This is brief.* HARRY *exits.* JACKMAN *enters the sunroom. He wears a shirt and tie, and carries a jacket, which he throws down.*)

MAHAVOLITCH: You hear the geese.

JACKMAN: I heard something. Is that what it was?

MAHAVOLITCH: About fifty of them. Took me straight back to the prairie—the sound of them.

JACKMAN: You miss it—the prairies.

MAHAVOLITCH: Yeah. When I hear that kind of thing, I do.

JACKMAN: You got those files in order?

MAHAVOLITCH: Almost.

(MAHAVOLITCH *returns to file selection.* JACKMAN *opens the 8 × 10 envelope given to him by* MICHAEL. *Draws out photographs and papers.*)

You think Ambassador Raymond killed this Russian?

JACKMAN: It's possible. Or maybe Mrs. Raymond.

MAHAVOLITCH: The wife could've done it?

JACKMAN: She might have. Never close a door till you're all the way through, Mahavolitch. Somebody killed the lad—(*He holds up a photo of Mischa.*)—it hardly matters who. The point is, he was killed because Harry Raymond is our ambassador. The thing we don't understand is—why did the Russians let him go?

MAHAVOLITCH: It was *them* who got in touch with the Minister? *Them* who said: "Take him home"?

JACKMAN: So we're told. But it doesn't make any sense.

MAHAVOLITCH: It's a set-up. He's an agent.

JACKMAN: Could be. Make it seem he's in trouble. Set us off on the wrong track. It could be.

(*He puts the photo down and picks up a file.*)

MAHAVOLITCH: You trust the Minister?

JACKMAN: Michael Riordon? I'd better. He called us in on this.

MAHAVOLITCH: That doesn't mean you can trust him, sir. (*Beat.*) I never did like his politics. High-falutin type. Left-leaning intellectual. Now, it looks like he's gonna be PM, for Christ's sake.

JACKMAN: That's right.

MAHAVOLITCH: Anti-American, too. Keeps pulling back from the Yanks. They're our allies, for Pete's sake, but he keeps pulling back. We got all their fucking deserters and all their fucking draft dodgers up here. Tolerated. Molly-coddled. There's got to be a reason. I figure it's guys like Riordon—guys like Raymond. "Come on over! We love ya!" Jesus.

JACKMAN: (*Amused.*) Someone should hire you as a border guard. Okay—let's get on with the business at hand. Potent stuff, this.

(JACKMAN *hands photographs over.*)

MAHAVOLITCH: (*Beaming.*) Phew! Yeah! Po-tent!

JACKMAN: You got it.

(*They become relatively immobile.* MARIAN *enters the garden and stands looking down from the jutting edge. One hand is fisted.*)

DIANA: (*Off.*) Mother?

(MARIAN *does not react. She might as well be deaf.* DIANA *comes along one of the walkways.*)

You have this knack for disappearing.

MARIAN: I'm right here.

DIANA: Aren't you going to eat any breakfast?

MARIAN: I've already had lunch.

DIANA: You can't have, Mother. It's nine in the morning.

MARIAN: Is it really?

DIANA: Yes. What's that in your hand?

MARIAN: Nothing.

DIANA: (*Laughing.*) Well—you seem to have a fairly tight grip on *nothing*, Mother. Show me what it is.

MARIAN: (*Turning away.*) No.

(MARIAN *pockets her hand.*)

DIANA: All right. (*Beat.*) What are you staring at down there?

MARIAN: People. Walking under the trees. (*Suddenly yelling.*) Get out from under my trees!

DIANA: Mother—for heaven's sake. You mustn't yell at people. It's rude. (*She looks over edge.*) I don't see anyone.

MARIAN: They left.

DIANA: Oh. Well.

MARIAN: If you want to get people out of your life, Diana—yell at them. (*She turns around and yells at the house.*) Get out of my life!

(JACKMAN *and* MAHAVOLITCH *look up.* MAHAVOLITCH *crosses to the windows.*)

JACKMAN: Who's yelling?

MAHAVOLITCH: It's her—out in the garden.

JACKMAN: The wife?

MAHAVOLITCH: Yeah. (*He smiles.*) She's really wacky, isn't she.

JACKMAN: (*Joining him.*) No. She's really scared. (*Beat.*) I kind of like the other one. The daughter.

MAHAVOLITCH: (*Leering.*) Yeah?

JACKMAN: Yes.

MAHAVOLITCH: You'd better watch it, Superintendent.

JACKMAN: I know what I'm doing.

MAHAVOLITCH: Oh, sure. When it comes to women, we all know what we're doing.

DIANA: Undo your hand, Mother. It's bleeding.

MARIAN: Is it?

DIANA: Yes.

(DIANA *comes round and sits beside* MARIAN. *She forces the fist open.*)

Good Lord. It's full of gravel . . .

(*She tips the gravel onto the ground and gets out a handkerchief.*)

MARIAN: I was looking for round, smooth stones. There weren't any.

DIANA: Oh, Mother . . .

MARIAN: (*Withdrawing her hand.*) It doesn't hurt. Leave it alone.

(*She wraps* DIANA*'s handkerchief around it.*)

DIANA: You should come in the house and let me wash it.

MARIAN: No. I will not go back in that house.

DIANA: All right. I'll go. I'll get some disinfectant.

(DIANA *exits.* MARIAN *reaches down and gathers some of the gravel. She stares at it.*)

MARIAN: (*Speaking the words.*) Back in Nagasaki—where the fellows chew tobaccy—and the women wicky-wacky—woo . . .

(*She lays down a single piece of gravel.*)

There. (*Beat.*) Someone else's move.

(MUSIC: *flute—Japanese.*
HARRY *enters the sunroom.*)

HARRY: Gentlemen. Forgive me. I'm late.

SCENE NINE

(*Morning. To one side, a table and two chairs in the Riordon household.* MICHAEL *seated, reading newspapers.* JULIET *checking her guest list. Coffee cups.*)

MICHAEL: (*Reading.*) FBI agents—This is the *Washington Post*—have established that the Watergate bugging incident stemmed from a massive campaign of political spying and sabotage conducted on behalf of President Nixon's re-election . . .

JULIET: Fascinating. But anything of interest?

MICHAEL: No.

(*He throws the* Washington Post *aside and picks up the* New York Times.)

JULIET: Have you read the Canadian papers yet?

MICHAEL: I read them second.

JULIET: I should have thought this morning you would have read them first.

MICHAEL: Why?

JULIET: Our friends, Michael. Our friends.

(LIGHTS *rise on* MARIAN *in her garden—still playing one-handed Go with stones on the bench.*)

MICHAEL: That won't be in the papers.

JULIET: Oh?

MICHAEL: Press blackout.

JULIET: At whose instigation? Yours?

MICHAEL: That's right.

JULIET: Don't you have to check that sort of thing through Cabinet?

MICHAEL: Sometimes.

JULIET: What about the PM?

MICHAEL: The PM is too ill to deal with this.

(MARIAN *places a stone.*)

JULIET: You mean you haven't even told him?

MICHAEL: Juliet—I know what I'm doing.

(MARIAN *sets another stone in place.*)

JULIET: Are you telling me no one knows he's here—in Ottawa? My god, Michael. You scare the hell out of me.

MICHAEL: Nonsense.

JULIET: Don't talk to me that way. I'm on your side.

MICHAEL: Then abide by the rules.

(MARIAN *sets down another stone.*)

JULIET: (*Shaken, she sits.*) You're acting on your own, aren't you. You brought them out of Russia on your own.

MICHAEL: You're conducting a one-sided conversation, Juliet.

JULIET: (*Sickened; quiet.*) You're acting on your own.

MICHAEL: Prattle.

JULIET: This is not prattle.

MICHAEL: It sounds like prattle to me.

JULIET: I *know* something.

(MICHAEL *looks over the* Times.)

I thought that might catch your attention.

(MICHAEL *carefully folds paper, lays it aside.*)

MICHAEL: Is there any more coffee?

JULIET: Help yourself.

(MICHAEL *rises, pours* [*imaginary*] *coffee from a pot on an* [*imaginary*] *sideboard.*)

MICHAEL: So? What is it you know?

JULIET: I know about the dead boy in the Moscow hotel.

(*Pause.* MARIAN *raises her hand—about to set another stone. She waits.*)

MICHAEL: (*Calmly.*) Interesting. How do you know about that?

JULIET: I'm not the only prattler in town, Mike.

MICHAEL: All right. Who was it?

JULIET: I never divulge names. (*She smiles at him.*) You told me to abide by the rules, my dear.

(MARIAN *sets the stone in place.* MICHAEL *returns to table, and sits.* JULIET *pushes at her guest list.*)

Do you mind if Mary Ann Turnbull sits on your left tonight?

MICHAEL: I think you had better sit on my left tonight.

JULIET: You really do take the cake. You're afraid I'll say something.

MICHAEL: Juliet . . .

(MICHAEL *picks up a paper and sets it aside.*)

JULIET: What I heard was—this dead young man might have been Marian Raymond's lover . . . That's the prattle.

MICHAEL: Is it, now.

JULIET: Yes, sir.

(*Pause.* MICHAEL *rises and walks away to a window.*)

MICHAEL: Juliet . . . I have a confession to make.

JULIET: Yes?

MICHAEL: I want to be Prime Minister. (*He looks at her.*) Do you understand what I'm saying?

(*Pause. She looks away.*)

JULIET: Yes. You're saying that—because of that dead young man in Moscow—you may have to throw our friends to the wolves. (*Beat.*) Because you want to be Prime Minister.

MICHAEL: Rule number one, Juliet: *one does what must be done.*

(JULIET *turns all the way from him.* LIGHTS *begin to fade.*

MUSIC: *flute rises.*
MARIAN *sets the final stone in its place.*)

SCENE TEN

(*Sunroom. Noon.* MAHAVOLITCH *is acting as feeder for* JACKMAN, *handing him various pieces of paper as* JACKMAN *speaks.* HARRY *is in a contained mode, showing little reaction to the questions—courteous, but reserved. Not cordial, but without hostility.*)

JACKMAN: Ambassador, were you ever associated with the Institute of Pacific Relations?

HARRY: Yes. Some years ago.

JACKMAN: Did you ever write for a magazine called *Amerasia*?

HARRY: Yes. I was once considered something of an expert on the subject of Japanese culture. I served there after the war. I'd been assigned to work with General MacArthur. He was a sort of *king*. Not yet an *emperor*, if you get my drift . . .

(MAHAVOLITCH *watches him, narrow-eyed.*)

JACKMAN: You worked with a fellow Canadian there . . . (*He pretends to look for a name.*) a man called . . . Norman.

HARRY: Herbert Norman. That's right. He was my boss. Technically, I'd been assigned to him—but his work was with General MacArthur. (*Beat.*) Superintendent—

JACKMAN: (*Cutting through.*) Herbert Norman was also an expert on Japan?

HARRY: Yes. He was *the* expert. He was born there. Of missionary parents.

JACKMAN: Your parents died . . . ? A car accident?

HARRY: Yes. When I was a child. An uncle raised me. My father's brother. (*Beat.*) Superintendent—it was my understanding I was here to talk about a death in Moscow.

JACKMAN: This is about a death in Moscow.

(*He snaps his fingers and accepts the next file from* MAHAVOLITCH.)

You were a student at Cambridge University?

HARRY: Yes. Kindness of my uncle. It had been my father's ambition for me.

JACKMAN: (*From a list.*) And your fellow students there were Donald Maclean—Guy Burgess—and Herbert Norman?

HARRY: Yes.

JACKMAN: Over the years, you and Ambassador Norman seem to have bumped into one another rather a lot. Clearly, you shared a number of interests. Would you care to elaborate?

HARRY: I've already told you—Herbert Norman was a revered Japanese scholar. I made some minor contributions on the subject. We often spoke of things Japanese.

JACKMAN: Nothing else?

HARRY: Nothing else.

JACKMAN: What about communist ideology?

HARRY: Stop this! Herbert Norman was not a Communist. That has been proven conclusively. Period. End of story.

JACKMAN: And you?

HARRY: There is no reason to doubt my loyalty, Superintendent.

JACKMAN: That sounds good, Ambassador. But—loyalty to what?

HARRY: My country.

JACKMAN: Well—if you say so . . .

HARRY: (*Losing his temper.*) I *know* so, Superintendent. *And so do you.* (*He cools.*) Get to the point. I want to know why I am here. And my wife. And my daughter. You still have told me absolutely nothing about that young man in Moscow.

JACKMAN: Okay. The point. (*Indicating a brown envelope.*) In here, there are photographs. (*He offers the envelope.*) Look at them.

HARRY: No.

(HARRY, *clearly alarmed, turns away.* JACKMAN *removes the photographs and offers them.*)

JACKMAN: Look at them!

HARRY: No.

JACKMAN: Ambassador Raymond—these photographs may not be pretty. They may not be uplifting. They sure as hell are not pleasant. But they are *evidence.*

HARRY: I'm sorry. I can't . . . I cannot look at him dead.

JACKMAN: (*Pause.*) Who says he's dead?

HARRY: He was murdered. The Minister said so . . . a hotel room in Moscow . . .

JACKMAN: Well—these may show a hotel room in Moscow, Ambassador, but . . . (*He looks at the pictures.*) the boy in here sure ain't dead. (*Beat.*) I could show them to your wife. See what she has to say . . .

(HARRY *sits down.*)

Maybe it would help if you spoke to her. Tell her what we have here.

HARRY: (*Long pause.*) Yes. I will speak to her. But I will not look at those photographs. I would rather be blind.

JACKMAN: Suit yourself.

HARRY: Thank you. May I go now?

JACKMAN: Yes, sir.

(HARRY *stands up. He is a bit lost. Turns the wrong way.* JACKMAN *points out the door.* HARRY *exits.*)

(*Calling after him.*) We will want to continue, Ambassador, this afternoon.

(JACKMAN *hands* MAHAVOLITCH *photographs.*)

Put these back in the envelope.

(*As he does this,* MAHAVOLITCH *turns one of the photographs sideways—and then upside down—and smiles.*
LIGHTS *fade.*
MUSIC: *flute.*)

SCENE ELEVEN

(*The garden*
MUSIC: *flute continues.*
HARRY *enters. He walks to the jutting edge and looks at the sky. He is afraid to look down.*)

HARRY: Mischa Andreevitch Bugarin . . .

(MARIAN *enters the garden, lost.* DIANA *enters. She crosses to the bench and, stooping behind it, begins to gather up* MARIAN'*s stones.* HARRY *looks at the audience.*)

Nineteen years old when he died . . .

(MARIAN *gets out her cigarettes.*)

DIANA: Everybody dies, Father.

HARRY: Yes.

(MARIAN *lights her cigarette.*)

But everyone isn't killed.

DIANA: (*Looking at him.*) Is that why you're here? They think it was you.

HARRY: That's right. Me.

(MARIAN *coughs—quietly.*)

DIANA: (*Having waited.*) Was it you? (*Beat.*) Daddy?

(DIANA *looks at* MARIAN.)

Mother? He was your friend. Who *was* he? Mischa?

HARRY: He was my lover, Diana.

(MUSIC *stops abruptly, mid-note.*

Nobody moves. LIGHTS *fade to black. End of Act One.*)

Act Two

*(MUSIC: piano. The MUSIC is vaguely "cocktail
lounge"—the sort of thing that might be played as people
gather for a party.*

*HARRY is seated on the garden bench. He now wears a
tweed jacket. MARIAN is seated in profile to the audience
on one of the upper levels. She wears a Japanese kimono as a
bathrobe. A small table contains a mirror and some make-up.
A cigarette burns in an ashtray. She is trying to locate the
person she can recognize as her "self." As she begins, there is
nothing on her face but matte. She will draw on the rest.
From time to time, she pauses to look at herself—and to
drink. On another of the levels, JULIET and MICHAEL
prepare for their party. MICHAEL, who will end up in
tuxedo and black tie, is dressed but for shirt buttons, tie, and
jacket. JULIET is dressed, but fixing her hair.)*

JULIET: How long have we been doing this . . . ?

MICHAEL: Since we began, I guess. 1943. Santiago—Chile.

JULIET: Our first posting. Dear me . . . we were children.

MICHAEL: Well—hardly.

JULIET: We were very, very green, Mike. We knew nothing . . .

MICHAEL: (*Pleasantly.*) Speak for yourself.

JULIET: I never speak for myself, my darling. I always speak for you.

MICHAEL: I was legal counsel, then. I liked that job.

JULIET: Yes. And weren't those the days. The war and everything . . .

MICHAEL: (*Cannot manage his cufflinks.*) Can you . . . ?

(JULIET *attaches the links.*)

JULIET: Some of it was screamingly funny. Remember? Chile was non-combatant. Neutral. And whenever the Ambassador's wife gave a dinner party, all the warring factions would have to be kept at a strategic distance from one another . . . all those pompous delegations in uniform . . .

MICHAEL: The Germans. Yes. The Italians . . .

JULIET: The Spaniards. All the fascists . . . (*Completes cufflinks.*) There you go. And of course, being in uniform, they came to the dinner parties armed to the teeth! The Ambassador's wife said this was intolerable.

She refused to allow the wearing of firearms at her
table. You remember this?

MICHAEL: No. I remember the men being in uniform—
but that's all.

JULIET: What she did was—oh, it was wonderful—she set
out squares of white lace beside all the wine glasses—
and the Germans, the Italians, the Spaniards were all
required to lay their pistols down on these . . . (*She
laughs.*) *gun-doilies*. That's what we called them. Gun-
doilies, my darling! Talk about diplomacy!

MICHAEL: Tie, please.

(JULIET *straightens his tie. He starts to move for his jacket.
She pulls him back—using his suspenders.*)

JULIET: Michael . . .

MICHAEL: Yes?

JULIET: Don't harm them. Our friends.

MICHAEL: Our guests are about to arrive.

JULIET: Michael—please.

MICHAEL: (*Freeing himself.*) Leave our friends to me,
Juliet. Don't interfere.

JULIET: What if it was us—in trouble?

MICHAEL: (*Putting on his jacket.*) It's not us. It's them.

JULIET: *Us*—and *them*. That sounds familiar, somehow.

MICHAEL: It's time, Juliet. Our guests . . .

(*He exits.*)

JULIET: (*Pause.*) It's time, Juliet. Our guests. Yes. And how will I get them to put their guns on the table . . .

(*She exits. Their* LIGHTS *fade*
MUSIC: *the piano alters.*
DIANA *enters the upper platform where* MARIAN *sits.*
MARIAN *sees her in the mirror.*)

MARIAN: Get out.

(DIANA *exits.* LIGHTS *fade on* MARIAN.)

SCENE TWO

(DIANA *goes to the sunroom via steps and walkways. A dog barks off in the distance.* MAHAVOLITCH, *in running shorts and sweatshirt, enters the garden.*)

MAHAVOLITCH: Hi, there.

HARRY: Hello.

MAHAVOLITCH: Great evening for it.

HARRY: Great evening for what?

MAHAVOLITCH: Running.

HARRY: Oh, Yes.

(DIANA, *in the sunroom, pours a drink for herself.*)

MAHAVOLITCH: You ever?

HARRY: Ever what?

MAHAVOLITCH: Get out there and pound the pavement.

HARRY: No.

MAHAVOLITCH: Nothing like it. Might do you some good. You never know.

HARRY: Somehow, I doubt it. I'm an old man, Corporal. Old men don't run.

MAHAVOLITCH: My old man did.

HARRY: Bravo.

MAHAVOLITCH: I'm from Regina. My old man used to park us on the prairie and both of us would get out and run. Ten miles and more.

HARRY: I envy you.

MAHAVOLITCH: Yeah?

HARRY: Yes. The distance.

DIANA: Father? (*To* MAHAVOLITCH.) Good evening.

MAHAVOLITCH: Hi.

DIANA: (*Coming down the steps.*) Do you think we could be alone for a moment, Corporal?

MAHAVOLITCH: Sure. I got to go and shower, anyway.

DIANA: He won't run away, I promise.

HARRY: You don't have to promise, Diana. I've already told him I'm too old. And not inclined.

MAHAVOLITCH: See you.

HARRY: Yes. Indeed.

(MAHAVOLITCH *exits.*)

SCENE THREE

(DIANA *crosses down stage.*)

HARRY: Before you speak, Diana, I have something to say.

DIANA: No. It's my turn to speak.

HARRY: What? Your summation. You haven't heard the whole case.

DIANA: This is not a "case," Father.

HARRY: You could have fooled me. You're being so aggressive, I'm surprised you're not wearing your gown. (*He rises.*)

DIANA: You want me to get it? Would it make you feel more secure? That way, at least, you could identify me.

(HARRY *crosses to the jutting edge.*)

That's right—walk away. I still recognize defensive behaviour when I see it. That I do recognize—but not much else.

HARRY: What does that mean?

DIANA: (*Letting it out.*) It means I don't know who you are!

HARRY: I'm your father. How do you do.

DIANA: Don't you dare demean the way I feel.

HARRY: (*Angrily.*) I love you, Diana.

DIANA: Tell me all about it!

HARRY: I love you. I love you. That's all I have to say.

DIANA: Is that what you said to Mother?

HARRY: You don't understand.

DIANA: Damn right I don't. Damn bloody right I don't. How can I? What am I supposed to understand? That all my life you've lied about who you are? That everything you said and did was a lie? (*Beat.*) God in heaven, Father—I don't care *what* you are. But I have a right to know *who* you are—who my father *is*.

I cannot begin to describe how I have admired you all these years. How profoundly I have admired you. I looked upon you—I told that man in there—I told him that I looked upon you with wonder. *Wonder*, Father. *God damn it.*

(*She almost loses control, but regains it.*)

It was always the thought of you, Father, that saved me

when other men battered me with their lies and self-deception. But I always knew they were lying. I always knew they deceived themselves about who they were and how righteous they were! They were bastards—every one of them! Every one of them *lied*. And they were so full of pride and self that most of the time they didn't even know they were lying.

Men are like that. Men are like that—but not you. Not you. You were whole. You were a whole man . . . true, above all other things, to yourself. I knew who you were. And now you want me to understand . . . I am given to understand . . . I am supposed to understand that I don't know you. All of a sudden—bam! An instant stranger. What am I going to do with this information, Father? Not that you're queer—who gives a damn! But that you lied. You lied. You lied like all the rest—and my problem is, I don't know where the lie begins—and I don't know where it ends.

HARRY: It ends where it began. There is nothing more to say. (*Beat.*) How the hell am I supposed to talk about this? What can I possibly tell you? This is not something that happened to you, Diana. It happened to me. And to your mother. *We* are paying for this—not you. Come down from your great, hurt place and the "privilege" of pain. It is unbecoming to you.

DIANA: Somehow, that doesn't bother me, Father. I still want to know who you are.

HARRY: I have nothing to say.

DIANA: What? Still in hiding?

HARRY: Silence is not a hiding place, Diana.

DIANA: It seems to have provided a pretty damn good hiding place for you.

HARRY: I am not in hiding. I am here. Right here—standing in front of you. *Me.*

(JACKMAN *comes onto a walkway, more in shadow than in light.*)

If you can't see me, Diana—tough.

(MARIAN *enters the sunroom, still wearing her robe. She pours herself a drink.*)

You say "who gives a damn" if I'm homosexual. *I do.* My *work* does. My government does. *Do not be a homosexual. Do not be a homosexual. Do not be that. Be anything—but do not be a homosexual.*

(JACKMAN *shifts his position slightly.*)

Tell me something, Diana. I'd be fascinated to know how you might defend me if the subject of who I really am were ever brought to trial. Eh? How would you do that?

(*No answer.*)

May I remind you *that silence is not a hiding place?*

DIANA: I can't answer that question.

HARRY: Yes, you can. Try.

(DIANA *turns away.*)

Frightened, are you? Scared. *God knows what else is hidden in here.* Is that it? *Me—the immoral seducer of hundreds—maybe thousands of young men? Me—the pervert? Me—the murderer?* (*Beat.*) Damn right, Diana. You don't know me. But not because I lied. You don't know me because you do not want to know *me*. You want to know a stranger. An invention.

DIANA: I did not invent you, Father. You invented yourself: *Harry Raymond—straight as a die!*

HARRY: (*Pause.*) Feeling better?

DIANA: Yes!

HARRY: Interesting, isn't it? You just revealed a prejudice you didn't know you had. (*Beat.*) Put it this way, Diana—say I had been out there where you and everyone else could see me. What would you have done with that? You, with your liberal ideals—how would you have explained me to your friends? Your lovers—your husbands? All those righteous bastards you consorted with. How would you have done that?

DIANA: (*Quietly.*) I could have said . . . I would have . . . said . . . (*She stops.*)

HARRY: (*Quietly.*) There you are, then.

DIANA: Yes. Here I am. I'm sorry, Father.

HARRY: How dare you be *sorry*. You—with your refusal to let people be. Why do you think they lied to you—all those men you hate? Your boyfriends, your lovers, your husbands—why do you think they lied? They lied because you would not let them be who they were. They had to lie in order to win you.

DIANA: I'm not a prize, Father.

HARRY: You're damn right you're not.

DIANA: Oh, please—why are we doing this?

HARRY: We're doing this because this is how people survive. We kill whatever stands in our way.

DIANA: You don't believe that.

HARRY: I killed what stood in my way, Diana. Stone dead.

(JACKMAN *shifts again.*)

DIANA: (*Pause.*) Are you telling me you killed this boy?

(HARRY *walks away from her.*)

Are you telling me you killed him?

HARRY: Do you never listen? I'm telling you I killed my self.

(MARIAN *lights a cigarette.*)

DIANA: But . . . then, why Mischa?

HARRY: Mischa . . . (*Pause.*)

(MAHAVOLITCH *walks onto one of the upper levels. He wears a towel around his waist—and is otherwise naked.* HARRY *speaks with genuine remembered affection, touched with the knowledge of Mischa's betrayal.*)

Mischa. Yes. (*Beat.*) When I saw him first, it was like those meetings you have in dreams, when a stranger greets you and you recognize him instantly. *You, is it? I've been waiting for you.* I was his Lazarus, he was my miracle worker. Rise up and walk. Rejoin the living . . .

(MAHAVOLITCH *removes the towel and dries his torso.*)

The living look so—beautiful, Diana. So unbearably
beautiful—to the dead.

DIANA: (*Pause.*) Were you lovers for very long?

HARRY: No. Less than a year. A matter of months.
Weeks. He was just very suddenly . . . *there.* We were
in the south, your mother and I. She was already ill,
probably had been for quite a while. But with
Alzheimer's—who knows when it begins? She was
tense. Tired. She kept forgetting where we were. Total
disorientation. She saw the palm trees and thought we
were in Cairo.

DIANA: And where were you?

HARRY: Yalta. It sits on a series of hills above the Black
Sea. It is where all good Russians go to recuperate.
There are baths there—the waters. Which is how we
met. In the baths. He walked right up to me and spoke
his name. Naked. I was lost. There was nothing I could
do. My defences—the whole castle—fell.

(MAHAVOLITCH *throws the towel to one side and begins
to dress.*)

DIANA: Why was he killed—if he was only your friend?

(HARRY *does not answer this.* JACKMAN *moves slowly along the walkway.*)

He died in Moscow. Was it you who brought him back there? From Yalta.

HARRY: No. I would not have dared do that. He came there on his own. It was a shock, I'm here to tell you, when he walked into my office one day and said, "Here I am." I met him on my holidays—he came to me on his. He was a student. Of acting. He wanted to be an actor.

(MARIAN *comes to the top of the sunroom steps.*)

MARIAN: (*As if to herself.*) My goodness! It's just like summer—an evening in August. Look at the moon. And everything is so still.

DIANA: What about Mother, Father?

HARRY: What about her?

DIANA: She's so distracted. Almost like someone adrift. Isn't there something I can do?

HARRY: I thought you would never ask, Diana. (*He smiles.*) Yes. You can get us something to eat.

DIANA: Mother? Are you hungry?

MARIAN: There's some chicken à la king in there. In cans.

DIANA: I'll go and heat it up.

(DIANA *crosses the garden to the steps, seeing* JACKMAN *as she goes.*)

Don't you ever go away?

HARRY: He can't go away, Diana. He's a part of us, now. The watcher—watching. The listener—listening, no doubt. Good evening, Superintendent.

JACKMAN: (*Turning.*) Yes, sir. Very pleasant.

HARRY: That's right. "Very pleasant." Saw nothing. Blind. Heard nothing. Deaf.

(MARIAN *comes down and sits on the bench with her drink.* DIANA *exits through the sunroom.*)

Have you eaten, Superintendent?

JACKMAN: Thank you. It's all arranged. We have a pizza coming in.

HARRY: With or without anchovies?

JACKMAN: With, Ambassador. *With.* Those of us from by the sea can't do without our salt.

HARRY: (*Moving towards the sunroom.*) I take it you will want me in the morning.

JACKMAN: No, sir. I will want you this evening—once you've dined.

(HARRY *goes up into the sunroom, turning for a brief look at* MARIAN. *Then he goes to pour himself a drink.*)

SCENE FOUR

(*The garden.* LIGHTS *come on in the sunroom as* HARRY *moves from lamp to lamp. The moonlight is intense.* JACKMAN *moves down into the garden.*
MUSIC: *from somewhere in the house, a radio can be heard. A record is being played of a sentimental song.*)

MARIAN: Have you come to ask me to dance?

JACKMAN: I don't think so, ma'am.

MARIAN: Why not? You've been dancing all day with my husband.

JACKMAN: Very well said, ma'am.

MARIAN: (*Looking at him.*) You're some kind of killer, aren't you.

JACKMAN: Oh—I don't think that's quite fair. I have my job to do. Same as you.

MARIAN: I have no job.

JACKMAN: Oh, I think you do, ma'am. Ambassador's wife—all that entails. You've had a long career of it, haven't you?

MARIAN: Long enough. How old do you think I am?

JACKMAN: It's not your age I'm interested in, Mrs. Raymond. It's your experience. What you remember.

MARIAN: I don't remember anything. Nothing. I can't seem to pull my mind into . . . (*She drifts.*)

JACKMAN: (*Pause.*) Focus, ma'am?

MARIAN: What?

JACKMAN: Your mind. You were saying . . .

MARIAN: I forget.

(*She rises, and crosses away from him.*)

JACKMAN: I was sort of hoping you could help me with some answers. The Minister, for instance. Mister Rior-

don. Is it true that he knew your husband when they
were both young men?

MARIAN: Yes.

JACKMAN: Where might that have been, Mrs. Raymond?

MARIAN: Somewhere. I don't know.

JACKMAN: Was it the war?

MARIAN: The war?

JACKMAN: The Second World War.

MARIAN: I was a cipher clerk.

JACKMAN: Yes. But your husband—your husband and
Mister Riordon . . .

MARIAN: They are not lovers, Superintendent.

JACKMAN: No, ma'am. I realize that. (*He gathers his
patience.*) Was it Michael Riordon who was Minister
when your husband received his posting to Moscow?

MARIAN: The posting came through the mail.

(*A doorbell rings, off.*)

Reinforcements have arrived. Yours, I believe.

(*Inside the radio is shut off.*)

What a pity. No more dancing.

JACKMAN: Yes, ma'am. Thank you. (*He realizes she has thwarted him.*) You dance—very well.

(MARIAN *drops him a mock curtsy.*)

I'm afraid I'll have to keep your husband busy for a while tonight.

MARIAN: Suit yourself. He's a grown man.

(MAHAVOLITCH *comes onto the walkway with a pizza box.*)

MAHAVOLITCH: Pizza's up.

JACKMAN: Yes.

(MAHAVOLITCH *exits.*)

Well, then . . .

MARIAN: Good evening.

JACKMAN: Good evening.

(JACKMAN *exits into the sunroom.*)

MARIAN: (*No emotion.*) Bastard.

(DIANA *enters.*)

DIANA: Mother? Food.

(MARIAN *waves her off. She drinks.* LIGHTS *change. In the sunroom,* MAHAVOLITCH *has joined* HARRY *and* JACKMAN.)

JACKMAN: In 1936, you were a student at Cambridge University.

HARRY: Yes. At Trinity College.

MAHAVOLITCH: Pizza?

JACKMAN: Thanks. Around that time, you were friendly with a young man named Francis Oliver.

HARRY: That's right.

JACKMAN: This Francis Oliver was a Socialist. Is that correct?

MARIAN: Don't.

HARRY: Actually, he called himself a Communist.

MARIAN: Don't.

JACKMAN: (*Checking a file.*) Francis Oliver was a good deal younger than you, was he not?

HARRY: Yes.

JACKMAN: What you might call a boy.

MARIAN: Make them stop. (*Yelling.*) Stop! Don't!

DIANA: (*Crossing to her.*) Mother—come in. *Now.*

MARIAN: (*Subsiding.*) Yes.

(*They begin to cross to the walkway exit as the garden* LIGHT *fades.*)

They don't know what they're doing to him. They don't understand what they're doing. (*Turning back.*) Stop!

(MARIAN *and* DIANA *exit.*)

SCENE FIVE

(*The sunroom.*)

JACKMAN: (*Eating pizza.*) It says here Francis Oliver was a well-known organizer of political meetings and (*Eating makes the next words unintelligible.*) left-wing demonstrations . . .

HARRY: Meetings and . . . ?

JACKMAN: (*Clearly.*) Left-wing demonstrations.

HARRY: Well—he was a Socialist, wasn't he. He was also a poet . . . That's what I remember. The poet.

JACKMAN: His mother was well-known, too. Dorothy Oliver wrote for the left-wing press. Then there was his great-grandfather. Charles Darwin . . .

HARRY: (*Amused.*) Another radical . . . Quite a family.

JACKMAN: (*Reading from the file.*) In 1937, Oliver left the Young Communist League . . .

HARRY: (*Waving his handkerchief.*) Hurray!

JACKMAN: . . . in order to become a full-fledged member of the Communist Party.

HARRY: Not "hurray." Presumably.

JACKMAN: Right you are, Mister Raymond. No "hurray" this time. Because it says here that in March of 1937—you, too, became a full-fledged Communist.

HARRY: Does it really? Well. What a pity.

MAHAVOLITCH: (*Referring to the file.*) Francis Oliver was quite a boy—according to this.

HARRY: Yes. He was.

MAHAVOLITCH: He had a lot of followers, it says here—you among them.

HARRY: I was his best friend. (*Pause.*) I adored him.

MAHAVOLITCH: Adored?

HARRY: Yes.

(JACKMAN *and* MAHAVOLITCH *exchange a look.*)

MAHAVOLITCH: Isn't that a strange thing to say about another man, Mister Raymond?

HARRY: I don't think so. I adored my uncle, too. And my uncle—by the way—was not a Communist.

JACKMAN: (*Checking a paper.*) He was a philosopher.

HARRY: He taught philosophy, Superintendent. There's a difference.

MAHAVOLITCH: Isn't communism a philosophy?

HARRY: It's a theory.

JACKMAN: There's a difference. (*He smiles.*) Now—about Francis Oliver. He was instrumental, then, in drawing you into the Communist Party?

HARRY: Francis Oliver could have drawn an angel into hell.

JACKMAN: But he drew *you* into the Communist Party.

HARRY: I went freely, Superintendent—happily, of my own accord. I approved of Marx. *Das Kapital* was a call to arms. I was young. It was a volatile world, back then, politically. Unlike today, the enemies of the people could be seen—identified—named. Hitler—Mussolini—Franco. Taking a stand against them seemed the only proper thing to do, for a young man with ideals.

(JACKMAN *refers to* MAHAVOLITCH*'s file.*)

JACKMAN: It says here that in 1938, Francis Oliver went to Spain.

(HARRY *turns away and walks to edge of the sunroom, facing the audience.*)

HARRY: Yes. He did.

JACKMAN: Where he fought in the Civil War on the Loyalist side.

HARRY: That's right.

JACKMAN: The Loyalists, at that time, were receiving aid from the Soviet Union. Yes?

HARRY: Correct. The whole of the Spanish Civil War was a Communist conspiracy.

MAHAVOLITCH: (*To* JACKMAN.) Who won?

HARRY: You did.

(MUSIC: *guitar. A Spanish sequence of chords.*)

MAHAVOLITCH: What happened? To Francis Oliver?

JACKMAN: (*Without emotion.*) He was killed. At Barcelona.

HARRY: December—1938. He was twenty years old. (*Pause.*) He died. I did not. He is dead. I am still here.

(*The* LIGHTS *fade.*

MUSIC: *concludes.*

MARIAN *enters the upper level—still wearing her robe.*
She prepares for bed. She carries a drink and the inevitable
cigarettes and lighter. In the sunroom, JACKMAN *and*
MAHAVOLITCH *are clearing files, etc.* HARRY *crosses*
to the drinks tray and takes up a bottle and glass. He holds up
the scotch.)

Sleep in a bottle. Goodnight, gentlemen.

JACKMAN: Goodnight, Ambassador. In the morning . . .

HARRY: Yes, yes. In the morning.

(HARRY *exits sunroom and begins to make his way via steps*
and walkways to the upper level where MARIAN *awaits him.*)

SCENE SIX

MAHAVOLITCH: Who the hell was this guy—Francis
Oliver?

JACKMAN: An idealist.

MAHAVOLITCH: So?

JACKMAN: So—he died for what he believed in. Don't
knock it. Let me show you something.

(JACKMAN *retrieves envelope of photographs. He removes some photographs and a second envelope from the first. He takes a single photo from the second envelope.*)

I've been saving this. Perhaps you'd better look at it now.

(MAHAVOLITCH *looks.* HARRY, *partway to his destination, pauses, out of breath.*)

MAHAVOLITCH: (*Obviously sickened.*) Holy shit . . . I don't want to see that.

JACKMAN: Hold it in your hand, Corporal. It's only a photograph.

(MAHAVOLITCH, *reluctant, does so.*)

There. A boy. A mere boy. What? Nineteen? Twenty?

(MAHAVOLITCH *lets photograph droop.*)

Look at it!

(MAHAVOLITCH *does so.*)

Not just at the picture, Corporal. Look at *him.* A portrait of commitment.

MAHAVOLITCH: He's dead.

JACKMAN: (*Harshly.*) Of course he's dead.

MAHAVOLITCH: (*Pause.*) Why?

JACKMAN: He believed. He was committed—one hundred per cent.

MAHAVOLITCH: You said he wanted to be an actor.

(HARRY *moves on.*)

JACKMAN: He was an actor. And a good one.

MAHAVOLITCH: You mean—he wasn't a homosexual? He was a plant, pretending to be queer?

JACKMAN: Sound familiar?

MAHAVOLITCH: It was all a scam. The usual.

JACKMAN: You've got it. Entrapment. Blackmail. They already had our friend Raymond's ideological sympathies. Once they had the photographs—he was all theirs.

MAHAVOLITCH: But he's our bloody ambassador!

(JACKMAN *ignores this and takes the photographs from* MAHAVOLITCH.)

JACKMAN: It worries me, though—the *double whammy*

aspect—the need to blackmail a man whose political history . . . (*Looking at the photographs.*) There's something still hidden in all of this. The dead boy—Mischa—why did he have to be killed? Just for a minute, I mean, assume the KGB did it.

MAHAVOLITCH: Kill their own person?

JACKMAN: Could be.

MAHAVOLITCH: But why?

JACKMAN: I don't know. It bothers me . . .

MAHAVOLITCH: You don't think Raymond did it to protect himself?

JACKMAN: Could be. It could also have been her—for the same reason.

MAHAVOLITCH: The crazy lady?

JACKMAN: Not crazy, Mahavolitch.

MAHAVOLITCH: I know, I know. She has . . . I forget.

JACKMAN: Alzheimer's disease.

MAHAVOLITCH: Yeah—affects the memory.

JACKMAN: Of course, in this instance, it may well have another name . . .

MAHAVOLITCH: Oh? What?

JACKMAN: *Loyalty.* Also affects the memory. Muddles the past. Forgets . . .

MAHAVOLITCH: You mean she's lying . . . pretending to be sick, just to protect *him?*

JACKMAN: Somebody killed this kid. Somebody had a reason. It's the reason that counts. Not who did it—but why. You learn that, once you've had to do it. Cold-blooded . . . (*Beat.*) I take it you have never killed, Mahavolitch.

(HARRY *enters the bedroom level.* MARIAN *puts out her hand in* HARRY's *direction.*)

MAHAVOLITCH: Not yet. No.

JACKMAN: You will. One day. I had to. Once.

(JACKMAN *replaces the photograph in the envelope.* HARRY *pours two drinks.*)

MAHAVOLITCH: Yeah?

JACKMAN: Yeah.

(*He gathers his topcoat from one of the chairs and puts it on.*)

MAHAVOLITCH: You're going out?

JACKMAN: I'm going out.

MAHAVOLITCH: Am I going with you?

JACKMAN: Of course not. Our guests. (*He starts to exit.*)

MAHAVOLITCH: Where are you going?

JACKMAN: To the boss. On a hunch.

(*He exits.* MAHAVOLITCH *picks up the envelope and looks at it. He takes out the photograph of Mischa dead and forces himself to look at it. The* LIGHTS *fade on* MAHAVOLITCH.)

SCENE SEVEN

(LIGHTS *rise on upper level area of* HARRY *and* MARIAN'S *bedroom.* MARIAN *is seated;* HARRY *is standing.*)

HARRY: It's all falling apart. It's all caving in . . .

MARIAN: Things fall apart. The centre will not hold . . .
   What happens to us now?

HARRY: We wait.

MARIAN: For what?

HARRY: Clarification.

MARIAN: Of what?

HARRY: Of how the universe intends to unfold. In the meantime, (*He raises his glass in a toast.*) we hold. (*He drinks.*)

MARIAN: To what, Harry? Hold to what?

HARRY: Us. To ourselves.

MARIAN: I don't know who I am, any more.

HARRY: (*As if he had not heard.*) We're not alone. We still have Mike.

(MARIAN *stares at him, afraid.* HARRY *turns and looks at her*)

Why the expression?

MARIAN: Nothing. Just something you said.

HARRY: What?

MARIAN: I don't know—just something you said. More, please . . .

(MARIAN *holds out her glass.* HARRY *pours them each a drink.* MARIAN *gives* HARRY *a radiant smile.*
MUSIC: *guitar—Spanish melody. Their* LIGHTS *fade.*)

SCENE EIGHT

(*Antechamber, Riordon household. A closed oak door.*
MICHAEL *and* JACKMAN. MICHAEL *is in evening dress.*

MUSIC: *piano—plus some chatter beyond the door.*)

MICHAEL: Well? What's so bloody urgent?

JACKMAN: We're making progress, sir. Some.

MICHAEL: You've shown him the photographs?

JACKMAN: I . . . tried.

MICHAEL: What do you mean?

JACKMAN: He refused to look at them.

MICHAEL: Have you told him what the compromising
  photographs reveal?

JACKMAN: (*With humour.*) He seems to know, sir.

  (SOUND: *there is a burst of party noise—someone has told
  a joke. Laughter beyond the closed door.*)

MICHAEL: What do you make of him, Superintendent?
  Do you think he did this dreadful thing?

JACKMAN: Which "dreadful thing" is that, sir?

MICHAEL: Why, the killing, of course. The boy. What else
  could I mean?

JACKMAN: The photographs—the blackmail. His homosexuality, sir. That's pretty dreadful in itself—given his
  high position.

MICHAEL: (*Warily.*) You think so, do you.

JACKMAN: I know so. What was he doing there, sir? In
  Moscow, of all places—an ambassador with homosexual tendencies. Sort of like tempting fate, isn't it—
  someone queer in such a sensitive position—when we
  all know they entrap the gay boys, drop of a hat. The
  easiest mark in town. Isn't that the way it goes?

MICHAEL: I was not aware of Ambassador Raymond's proclivities, Superintendent. If I had been, I would hardly have placed him in jeopardy.

JACKMAN: *Him*, sir? Or the country?

MICHAEL: I beg your pardon?

JACKMAN: I'm not accusing you, Minister. It's just—you must be aware the Americans are very hot on this subject. They've been on to us through the CIA, insisting the RCMP root out and remove all homosexuals from sensitive areas. The fact is, they would like to see us get rid of all homosexuals in government, period.

MICHAEL: Not much hope of that.

JACKMAN: (*With humour.*) If we could clear them out of External, the CIA would be satisfied.

MICHAEL: Would they, now.

JACKMAN: That's why I brought in Corporal Mahavolitch, sir. It's part of his unit's mandate—rooting out homosexuals. Normally, of course, we would pass whatever we find on to the Solicitor General. But in Ambassador Raymond's case—well . . . You brought us in on this yourself, didn't you, sir.

MICHAEL: (*Carefully.*) Yes. I did.

JACKMAN: Well, now—I haven't asked why that should be, sir. Have I.

MICHAEL: (*Carefully.*) No. You haven't.

JACKMAN: And I won't. Will I. I just thought it should be said: reiterated. You and me—we have *an understanding.* Am I correct?

MICHAEL: Yes. We have an understanding. (*Pause.*) Before you go, Superintendent—I think you should know a communiqué has arrived. From Moscow.

JACKMAN: Oh?

MICHAEL: They don't want him back. The Soviets.

(*He hands the paper to* JACKMAN, *who reads it as* MICHAEL *continues.*)

As you can see, the wording is subtle—"not at this time . . . as we await developments at your end . . . "

(JACKMAN *folds the page and hands it back to* MICHAEL.)

My fear is—a bargain has already been struck—an arrangement has already been set in motion as a result of this boy's death. Clearly, time is of the essence. All we know is—a young man lies dead in Moscow—was murdered brutally—was Harry Raymond's lover, whore, whatever—and now, they "await developments" at our end.

JACKMAN: Yes, sir.

(*Beyond the door, someone is making a humorous tribute to* MICHAEL. JACKMAN *turns to listen.*)

MICHAEL: So far, you tell me, nothing has been forthcoming. I want results—"Developments." And that is *your* job.

JACKMAN: Are you sure, sir?

MICHAEL: Absolutely!

JACKMAN: Are you sure the developments they refer to are all up to me? Or . . .

MICHAEL: Or what?

JACKMAN: It just occurred to me, sir—they could be referring to developments in there, sir. (*Off-stage.*) The Prime Minister's condition—the transference of power.

MICHAEL: Thank you, Superintendent, for your insight. And now—if you will excuse me . . . good night.

JACKMAN: Yes, sir. Thank you, sir.

(JACKMAN *exits.* LIGHTS *rise on upper level area of Harry and Marian's bedroom.* MARIAN *is seated;* HARRY *is standing.*)

MUSIC: *guitar evokes memories of heat*

MARIAN: Cairo. Cool white balconies—red tile floors. And ceiling fans . . . Tall frosted glasses full of lemonade or . . .

HARRY: Pimms. I remember the Pimms. Slices of cucumber, strawberries . . .

MARIAN: Harry?

(HARRY *and* MARIAN *exit.*)

SCENE NINE

(*The antechamber.* MICHAEL *is alone. He steps toward the exit. The party noises rise. He pauses in the light spill of the "doorway"—a silhouette, frozen. Slowly, he steps back, turns, and faces the audience. He removes his handkerchief from his trouser pocket—unfolds it—stares at it—raises it to his face—dries his forehead and, dabbing at his lips, stands again frozen—the handkerchief hanging down from his fingers.*)

JULIET: (*Off.*) Mike? Michael?

(MICHAEL *reanimates. He straightens—and makes a show of drying the back of his neck and the palms and backs of his hands. He does all this slowly.* JULIET *enters—carrying a red rose.*)

Oh, my darling—oh, my dear one! *We are on our way!* Straight to the top—where we belong. What was it Hamlet said?

MICHAEL: Hamlet said a lot of things, Juliet. Which did you have in mind?

JULIET: *The readiness is all.* Yes? The readiness is all—and we are *ready!* That whole room in there is primed to offer you the crown, Mike.

(*More off-stage* SOUNDS *of celebration.*)

Listen to them. Listen to them. And it's all for you. A triumph. Every single person we invited—every single one of them answered the call.

(*Off-stage* MUSIC *is heard.*)

Sometimes, I think what a pity it is more people aren't allowed to see how it's all made to work. The ingenuity—the artfulness—the wiliness—the subterfuge. The skill, my darling, which makes it all seem inevitable. The strategies. The machinations. Yes—the underhand-

edness—but oh—the finesse! We've come such a long,
long way—and we're *here!*

MICHAEL: Yes. Here we are.

JULIET: Survival of the fittest—yes? We've survived it all.
Unlike some . . . I can't get them out of my mind. Harry.
Marian. It's as if they'd ridden with us all the way to
the top beside us—and then fell back. Stricken. Inca-
pable. Wounded. (*She brightens.*) You remember the
four of us together? (*She laughs.*) People used to think I
was having an affair with Harry . . .

(MICHAEL *snorts.*)

Don't be so smug. People also thought you were having an affair with Marian.

MICHAEL: What will they think of next?

JULIET: Oh—I don't know. (*She shows the rose.*) That I'm
having an affair with the PM. (*Beat.*) The thing is—no
one will ever know about people like us. We're too well
hidden, our crowd. The diplomatic corps. Make a picture of it, Mike. All of us standing there together. None
of our eyes revealing anything—none of our mouths
betraying a trace of regret or of pain. The way we stand.
The way we allow ourselves to be seen but never known.
The way—in public—we *hold* ourselves. The way we

111

hold our glasses. The way we hold our liquor. The way we hold our tongues. The way we dress. The way we present our "persons." No privacy. No private lives. No lives at all, that one can see. But always—always there to be of service. I like to believe that's what the "external" in External Affairs describes—our talent—our aptitude—our *genius* for survival. (*Beat.*) Except . . .

(*There is the* S O U N D *of applause and laughter from beyond the door.* J U L I E T *is distracted by it.*)

M I C H A E L : Except . . . ?

J U L I E T : Not all of us survive.

(*More applause—approving laughter.*)

Were you aware that Harry Raymond once had a breakdown?

M I C H A E L : Breakdown? No. When?

J U L I E T : In Cairo. Back in the fifties, when Harry was ambassador to Egypt. Didn't you know? Marian told me.

M I C H A E L : No. I never knew about it.

J U L I E T : I probably shouldn't have told you. A breakdown should be private. Apparently Juliet nearly lost him— that's how bad it was. Poor man.

(*Off-stage, some of the guests have started rhythmic clapping.*)

I guess we should go back.

MICHAEL: Yes.

(*The clapping increases.* JULIET *looks at* MICHAEL *and smiles.*)

JULIET: It's you they want, now.

MICHAEL: Yes.

JULIET: Give me your hand, then.

(*The clapping is now very loud.* JULIET *leads* MICHAEL *to the door. There is a burst of applause.*)

You first!

(MICHAEL *exits.* JULIET *pauses—only for a moment. She hurries back to the mirror. Seeing herself, she thinks of the consequences of what is taking place. She thinks of* HARRY *and* MARIAN. *And then she turns her back on them—and follows* MICHAEL *into what has now become cheering. Party noises rise.*

MUSIC: *guitar, a chord. Then flute joins in: crossover to the past.*)

SCENE TEN

(*Upper level.* HARRY *and* MARIAN. LIGHT *patterns alter—a suggestion of louvered shutters. In the garden,* DIANA *appears, wearing her topcoat. She sits on the bench.* MARIAN *is seated at her little table. She turns on a lamp.*)

MARIAN: (*Younger.*) Tell me what happened today, Harry.

HARRY: (*Younger.*) Everything. Nothing.

MARIAN: (*Rising.*) More of everything than nothing, I suspect. I've never seen you work so hard.

HARRY: I don't mind the work. I thrive on it.

MARIAN: You may think you thrive on it, my darling— but it's really the other way round: *work thrives on you.* You look like the walking dead.

(MARIAN *crosses up stage and they both unloop the ties that have restrained a cloud of mosquito netting. The netting falls.* MARIAN *gathers up one end and creates a swatch, as if over a bed.*)

Just when we get to be Ambassador to Egypt, the whole Middle East explodes. So tell me—what did you do today?

HARRY: The Americans have landed troops in Lebanon. I spent a whole day with Colonel Nasser—trying to rein him in.

MARIAN: Come and sit down.

HARRY: (*Sits.*) Marines in Beirut. That lovely city . . .

MARIAN: I know.

HARRY: All our peace-keeping efforts gone up in smoke.

MARIAN: I know.

HARRY: (*Conjuring.*) It seems I'm doomed to work in a world run by military madmen. In Japan, it was General MacArthur. Where he lived—do you remember?— there was a garden. An ancient, civilized Japanese garden. With raked sand to walk in. It was so quiet there . . .

MARIAN: Yes. I remember.

HARRY: MacArthur never raised his voice. Not ever. During the Korean war, in that garden, he would whisper: "My air force will cut their troops to pieces. My bombs will decimate their people. Their cities will lie in ruin . . ."

MARIAN: (*Whispering.*) Yes.

HARRY: All my working life, I said: no. *No.* That's why diplomacy exists. That's what it's for. *No. Don't.*

MARIAN: Yes.

HARRY: (*Beat.*) Having had your say—knowing MacArthur has not even bothered to listen—you rise to leave him and walk away across the sand. And then this man comes out—gardener—Japanese—and he rakes away your imprint. It is just as if you had never been there.

(MARIAN *goes to her table and pours him another drink— and one for herself.*)

Now—this. Another General—President Eisenhower—has sent the Marines to Beirut.

(MARIAN *laughs.*)

It's funny?

MARIAN: No. But I just had this image of a boatload of Japanese gardeners going in after the troops to rake away their footprints.

HARRY: Oh, god. (*He suddenly weeps.*)

MARIAN: Don't, Harry. Don't. Please—please. Come to bed and rest.

HARRY: (*Rising, angry.*) I don't want to rest. I will not rest. Have I not made myself clear? Is something missing here? I have a job to do. I'm a diplomat. A peacemaker. God dammit! I want to work. I want . . . (*He moves away and leans on her table.*) I want—I must—I have to work.

MARIAN: Your work is killing you.

HARRY: Don't try to manoeuvre me out of the one thing I can do.

MARIAN: No one's manoeuvring you anywhere. I'm merely suggesting that you stop for a moment. Give yourself the benefit of doing something for *you*—for Harry. Pause. Breathe. Take a day off. Good Lord, you have lots of talented people on your staff—why not give them a chance? You never let anyone else do anything.

HARRY: I can't.

MARIAN: Maybe you can't. But you will.

HARRY: I must work . . .

MARIAN: No, Harry. Sleep. The least you can do is try. Please.

HARRY: It won't . . . I can't . . .

MARIAN: Yes, you can. Go.

(HARRY *goes behind the netting.* MARIAN *watches after him. When he is gone, she lights a cigarette and faces the audience.*)

(*Singing to herself.*) Back in Nagasaki . . . where the men all chew tobaccy . . . and the women . . . (*She stops.*) Harry?

(MARIAN *turns and goes behind the netting.* LIGHTS *dim.*)

SCENE ELEVEN

(*The garden. Morning. Sunlight.* DIANA *is seated on the bench, as before, but she has removed her topcoat and now lays it on the bench beside her.* MAHAVOLITCH *passes her, wearing running gear. Exits.* MARIAN *enters from one of the walkways. She wears a pale dress and sunglasses.* HARRY *paces on the upper level.*)

DIANA: How did you sleep?

MARIAN: I dreamt. I think I dreamt. I don't know. Cairo—Spain. I don't remember. All night long—somewhere else. (*Beat.*) It's hot.

DIANA: Yes. Indian summer.

(MARIAN *walks to the jutting edge.*)

MARIAN: Dog?

DIANA: No. No dog.

(JACKMAN *enters the sunroom, sees they are in the garden and goes about his business.*)

MARIAN: (*Litany.*) Nagasaki—Mexico City—Athens—
  Cairo . . .

DIANA: Quite a journey, Mother. You did it well.

MARIAN: Did we?

DIANA: Yes. I was very proud of you.

MARIAN: I keep thinking—there's something I must do.
  (*Pause.*) In Cairo . . . there was . . . (*She stops.*)

DIANA: Mother? In Cairo? What.

MARIAN: A young man. I . . . Something.

(MUSIC: *guitar. Step chords follow her through the following like a shadow.*)

  Your father. In Cairo. The staff was made up entirely of
  men and boys . . . cooks, gardeners, drivers. The boys

were messengers, mostly. Seventeen, eighteen years
old, who lived all their lives in the streets. Desperate,
all of them, for money. We used them as runners. Mes-
sages. Errands. There was . . . It was a time of crisis. A
diplomatic crisis. Almost a war. There had been an
assassination. The Americans had landed troops. The
tension was palpable. Your father . . . (*Beat.*) There was
a secretary. I can't remember his name. One of those
blond men with eyes like blue ice. Efficient enough—
but dangerous. He always wore a white linen suit—but
there was something secretive about him—hidden.
Then I found out what it was.

(M A R I A N , *using the present, conjures the past. The garden
becomes a courtyard in Cairo.*)

In the courtyard, there was a shed. This happened in
the afternoon . . . The sun was blazing. I'd gone to the
courtyard, thinking—I don't know—that I'd sit in the
shade and read. But there was no shade. Then I remembered an umbrella—a sort of beach umbrella—the kind
you stick in the sand. And I thought—well, it's in the
shed . . .

(M A R I A N *re-enacts the way she went into the shed—open-
ing the "door" with her arm. She removes her sunglasses.*)

The sun had blinded me. I couldn't see. I heard a
noise—but I couldn't see what it was. And then I could.

(DIANA *watches.*)

One of the messenger boys—a runner—was standing
in the shadows. His back was to the wall. His eyes—I
can still see his eyes. He was in some kind of ecstasy.
And . . . the blond young man—the secretary—was
kneeling in front of him . . . down on his knees in his
white linen suit. I didn't understand, at first. And then I
did. (*She puts the sunglasses back on.*) I turned and left
them without a word. I don't really know if the secretary knew I was there. But the runner—he knew. His
eyes had shown me that. And it was then—because I
had seen his eyes—that I knew how I could save your
father. Rescue him from the danger he was in. I could
bring the runner to him. Offer him to your father. After
all his years of silence and suffering, "Here," I could
say, "is the answer to your pain, Harry."

DIANA: And you *did* this?

MARIAN: You don't understand, Diana. I was living with
a man who was dying—of denial. Do you know what
that does? It kills. And I had to save his life. *I* could not
save it—not as me alone. Not any more. Not in that
moment. Your father loves me, Diana. But I alone was
not the answer to his pain. (*Beat.*) In Yalta, some years
later, I also led him to Mischa Andreevitch Bugarin . . .

DIANA: (*Pause.*) Why?

MARIAN: Why?

DIANA: Why did you bring him . . . men?

MARIAN: Love, Diana, does what it must. (*Beat.*) I would kill for him. If I had to.

SCENE TWELVE

(*The garden and upper level. Morning. Sunlight.* MARIAN *and* DIANA *stay in place.* MAHAVOLITCH *enters, having run.*)

DIANA: Good morning.

MAHAVOLITCH: Yeah. Great.

DIANA: I'm going to get some coffee, Mother. Do you want some?

MARIAN: Coffee? No.

(DIANA *exits, passing through the sunroom.* JACKMAN *steps forward, but she carries on without comment.* MAHAVOLITCH *moves into the garden area—where he begins to do some rudimentary end-of-run exercises, ignoring* MARIAN, *who seems to be lost in her own thoughts. Pause.*)

Is it your policy, Corporal, not to speak to strangers?

MAHAVOLITCH: (*Exercising.*) No, ma'am.

MARIAN: To women wearing . . . (*She looks at her dress.*) beige, perhaps?

MAHAVOLITCH: No, ma'am.

MARIAN: (*Removing her glasses.*) Women whose eyes you cannot see?

MAHAVOLITCH: No, ma'am.

MARIAN: Why is it, then?

MAHAVOLITCH: Why is what, ma'am?

MARIAN: That you won't speak to me. Do I frighten you?

MAHAVOLITCH: (*Stopping his exercise.*) No, ma'am.

MARIAN: (*Pause.*) Are you a married boy?

MAHAVOLITCH: No, ma'am. And I'm not a boy, Mrs. Raymond. Anything but. I'm thirty years old.

MARIAN: Heavens! An ancient. Thirty! (*Beat.*) And not married.

MAHAVOLITCH: No, ma'am.

(MARIAN *takes out a cigarette package.*)

MARIAN: Not inclined? Or just not ready . . . ?

MAHAVOLITCH: I think that's . . . I don't think that's any
of your business, Mrs. Raymond.

MARIAN: (*Has selected a cigarette.*) You don't.

MAHAVOLITCH: No, ma'am.

MARIAN: Have you a light, Corporal?

MAHAVOLITCH: I don't smoke.

MARIAN: Of course not. I wasn't thinking. (*She lights the
cigarette.*) I dare say there's quite a lot you don't do . . .

MAHAVOLITCH: (*A touch of anger.*) Ma'am?

MARIAN: You have wonderful legs.

(MAHAVOLITCH *is thrown by this.*)

Beautiful. In fact—you're a rather splendid specimen.
(*Pointedly.*) Aren't you.

(MAHAVOLITCH *is rooted, alarmed.*)

What? Have I found you out?

MAHAVOLITCH: I don't understand you, Mrs. Raymond.

MARIAN: Yes, you do. Leave my husband alone.

MAHAVOLITCH: What? (*He almost laughs.*) You must be . . .

MARIAN: *Leave him alone!*

(MAHAVOLITCH *stares at her, then turns and begins to exit. Simultaneously,* DIANA *enters sunroom.* MARIAN *speaks to* MAHAVOLITCH.)

Don't you dare do that.

(MAHAVOLITCH *stops — his back to* MARIAN. DIANA *enters garden.*)

I haven't lived . . . I haven't worked all this time . . . (*She begins to falter badly.*) We've worked so hard. It's been so . . . difficult . . .

DIANA: Mother?

(MAHAVOLITCH *moves away.* DIANA *looks at him.*)

MAHAVOLITCH: I was just leaving.

(MAHAVOLITCH *exits, with a final look at* MARIAN.)

DIANA: Are you all right?

MARIAN: (*Not all right.*) Yes.

DIANA: What happened?

MARIAN: Nothing happened. I lost . . . I've lost . . .

DIANA: Can I help? What have you lost?

MARIAN: Something. I don't know. I've lost something . . .

SCENE THIRTEEN

(*On the upper level,* MAHAVOLITCH *enters the room where* HARRY *sits at* MARIAN*'s table.*)

MAHAVOLITCH: Sir?

HARRY: (*Not looking at him.*) Time, gentlemen. Is that it?

MAHAVOLITCH: Yessir. (*Beat.*) Is there something I could do for you, Ambassador?

HARRY: Yes. You and your friend could leave this house.

MAHAVOLITCH: You know we can't do that, sir. (*He starts to exit.*)

HARRY: Young man . . . ?

MAHAVOLITCH: Sir?

(*In the garden,* MARIAN *discovers her umbrella is missing.* HARRY *stares at* MAHAVOLITCH.)

HARRY: . . . I'll be with you presently.

MAHAVOLITCH: Sir.

(MAHAVOLITCH *exits.* DIANA *looks for umbrella.*)

HARRY: So . . . (*He pours himself a drink.*) One: Never drink in a crisis. (*He drinks.*) Two: Never admit there is a crisis. (*Drinks.*)

(*Hold.*
MUSIC: *flute song.*)

SCENE FOURTEEN

(The garden and the sunroom. DIANA *enters the sunroom. The moment she is inside,* JACKMAN *withdraws the envelopes of photographs from her view and holds them.)*

JACKMAN: I think you'll find it just there. *(The umbrella.)*

DIANA: *(Finding it.)* Thank you.

JACKMAN: She's a great one for making up the rain—isn't she—your mother.

DIANA: This time, it's the sun—and if you look, Superintendent, you'll see that it's really there.

(She starts to exit.)

JACKMAN: Mrs. Marsden?

(DIANA stops.)

I'm sorry.

DIANA: No, you're not, Superintendent. But thank you for saying so.

(DIANA exits.)

JACKMAN: Damn.

(HARRY *enters the sunroom.* JACKMAN *is unaware of him. He looks at the envelope of photographs—and sighs.*)

HARRY: Something troubles you, Superintendent?

JACKMAN: Oh. Good morning, sir. Yes—these photographs . . .

(DIANA *hands the umbrella to* MARIAN. *They exit.*)

HARRY: I presume you have no taste for what they depict. I apologize.

JACKMAN: I've seen worse.

HARRY: I should hope so.

JACKMAN: What did they want of you, sir—in exchange for these?

HARRY: They wanted me to tell them how to make an atomic bomb.

JACKMAN: Please, sir . . .

HARRY: What else would they want, Superintendent? I don't know why—but I have a pervasive feeling of another time and place. I keep expecting Igor Gouzenko to walk through that door . . .

THE STILLBORN LOVER

(*Pause.* MAHAVOLITCH *enters, still in running gear.*)

MAHAVOLITCH: Sorry to be so long. I was . . .

HARRY: Never apologize, Corporal. Never explain.

JACKMAN: (*Pause.*) All right, Ambassador. I think the time
has come for you to look at these.

(JACKMAN *hands one photo envelope to* HARRY.)

Take your time.

(HARRY *crosses away from him. He undoes the envelope
and pulls out the pictures. He shuffles through them quickly,
barely looking.*)

HARRY: I've already seen these, Mister Jackman. In
Moscow some time ago.

JACKMAN: I think you may not have seen them all, sir.
There is one more. Here.

(JACKMAN *hands over the second envelope.* HARRY,
fearful of what he will see, turns away to open it. JACK-
MAN *watches him.*)

HARRY: Oh . . . god . . .

(*Suddenly*, HARRY *sits. Clearly, he had not known how Mischa died. The dog barks down in the ravine.*)

JACKMAN: Would you like a drink, Ambassador?

HARRY: Yes.

(JACKMAN *indicates* MAHAVOLITCH *should take it to him. When* MAHAVOLITCH *holds out the drink,* HARRY *stares at him.*)

It's not right, you know. It's not right. No one should do such things.

MAHAVOLITCH: This is for you, sir.

HARRY: Thank you. (*He takes the glass and drinks.*) In answer to your question, Superintendent—they wanted me to be their advocate here in Ottawa. It was known I would soon be returning home. They showed me the photographs—the other ones—those. The shock was not what the photographs revealed. It was not as if I was unaware of what I had done—with Mischa. The shock—the shock was that he was one of them. One of theirs. Not his own person, but someone else's person all along. That was the shock.

JACKMAN: I'm afraid it's somewhat worse than that, sir.

HARRY: Oh? How could it be?

JACKMAN: Were you not aware—are you not aware now—of your wife's part in all this?

HARRY: I beg your pardon.

JACKMAN: Your wife, Ambassador. It was she who . . . provided you with Mischa.

HARRY: (*Pause.*) You're crazy.

JACKMAN: I'm afraid not, sir.

HARRY: You are crazy.

JACKMAN: No, sir. She said so herself.

HARRY: When?

JACKMAN: This morning.

HARRY: To you?

JACKMAN: She said it in the garden, sir. I have it right here, on this tape.

(*He shows a micro-recorder.*)

HARRY: You are, of course, no better than them.

JACKMAN: Yes, sir.

HARRY: (*Looking at Mischa dead.*) Are you telling me that my wife . . . What are you telling me?

JACKMAN: I merely repeat what she said. Which suggests that your wife may have been acting in conjunction with the KGB to engineer their blackmail.

(HARRY *stares at him in disbelief.*)

Nothing is impossible, sir—given the stakes.

HARRY: Nonsense! That is absurd. I had a chance encounter with Mischa in the baths at Yalta. How is it possible my wife had even met him?

JACKMAN: Well, sir, I can only suggest she knew where to look—and there he was.

HARRY: You mean he was a prostitute?

JACKMAN: More than likely. Standing on his corner— young, attractive. Waiting.

HARRY: What you are describing, Mister Jackman, is grotesque. It is *crazy*. My wife would never betray me. Not ever.

(JACKMAN *watches* HARRY *work his way through the details.*)

I insist that—whatever she may have said—whatever she may have done—I insist that you withdraw your accusation that my wife acted in conjunction with the KGB. *I insist.* It is impossible even to begin to imagine it.

JACKMAN: Yes, sir. Accusation withdrawn. With apologies. (*Beat.*) Nevertheless, for whatever reasons, it was Mrs. Raymond who chose Mischa—and who sent him to the baths.

HARRY: And he was a plant from the KGB?

JACKMAN: Yes, sir. Well—if not a plant on the payroll, then certainly "plantable" for a fee. It's in the nature of it, isn't it, sir.

HARRY: In the nature of what?

JACKMAN: Prostitution.

HARRY: How would I know? It's more in your line of work than mine.

JACKMAN: Sorry, Ambassador. I've never used a prostitute in my life.

HARRY: Like hell, you haven't. There's one standing right beside you.

MAHAVOLITCH: Hey!

JACKMAN: I think that's uncalled for, sir.

HARRY: Tell him to put his clothes on. (*To* MAHAVOLITCH.) I'm not interested in young men wearing purple running shorts.

JACKMAN: (*Quietly.*) Go and get dressed.

MAHAVOLITCH: But . . .

JACKMAN: *Now.*

MAHAVOLITCH: Yes, sir.

(*He exits.*)

HARRY: You all work the same ploy, don't you. I guess it's in the nature of it, isn't it.

JACKMAN: (*Ignoring the insult.*) You still have not told me—we still have not discussed your answer, sir.

HARRY: What answer?

JACKMAN: The answer you gave the Russians—when they showed you the photographs.

HARRY: I said "no."

(JACKMAN *does not respond.*)

Do you think if I had said "yes," they would have done this to him?

(HARRY *hands the photograph of the dead Mischa to* JACKMAN, *who regards it sadly.* HARRY *crosses away.*)

That's what baffles you, isn't it, Superintendent. You must have guessed I'd said "no"—otherwise why would they kill him?

(MICHAEL *enters.*)

MICHAEL: All right, Superintendent. That will be all.

JACKMAN: (*Registering no surprise.*) Yes, sir.

MICHAEL: I'd like a moment alone with Ambassador Raymond. Would you mind?

JACKMAN: No, sir. Not at all.

(JACKMAN *exits past* MICHAEL.)

SCENE FIFTEEN

(*When* JACKMAN *is gone,* MICHAEL *moves downstage.*)

HARRY: Michael. (*Beat.*) How was your party?

MICHAEL: An unqualified success—according to Juliet.

HARRY: Why are you here, Mike? Aren't they moving fast enough for you?

MICHAEL: Frankly—no. I need answers. I'm being pressed.

HARRY: The PM?

MICHAEL: No.

(*When he does not elaborate,* HARRY *shrugs.*)

HARRY: I see. Pressure from without, is that it? (*Beat.*) Still no answer? My, my. So?

MICHAEL: You let me down, Harry. I had no idea you were so vulnerable.

HARRY: Are you going to moralize?

MICHAEL: No. But I have a right to register surprise. And disappointment. I trusted you. You were the best man I had. Then *this*.

HARRY: What do you think I've done? What can you possibly think I have done?

MICHAEL: I was not aware of what you are, Harry. I was not aware of your homosexuality.

HARRY: Good.

MICHAEL: Not good. How can I say I've known you for years if I did not know that?

HARRY: Everyone has secrets. You have secrets.

MICHAEL: None that would jeopardize my country.

HARRY: (*Pause.*) I see. So—what is to be done?

MICHAEL: There are options. We must weigh them.

(HARRY *sits on bench.*)

You could be returned to Moscow—stand trial for the murder of this boy. That is option number one.

HARRY: (*Tired.*) I did not kill him.

MICHAEL: How would you prove it?

HARRY: I could prove it with your help. If you threw the

weight of the whole department behind me—if you insisted on an open trial—if the P M spoke out . . .

MICHAEL: No.

HARRY: No? You know I didn't kill him! Help me. That's your job!

MICHAEL: (*Dreadful, reasoned calm.*) My job is to protect our integrity abroad. Such a trial would be a scandal, Harry. One we cannot afford. We are in a state of transition here. The P M's health—the transference of power . . .

HARRY: What is the other option?

MICHAEL: You stay here—and confess.

HARRY: I did not kill him.

MICHAEL: No. You confess to having submitted to black-mail—and to having . . . (*Carefully.*) foregone your oath of office.

HARRY: No! You are asking me to confess to something I did not do. Why can't you simply retire me? Recall me on compassionate grounds—because of Marian.

MICHAEL: What—and pretend that nothing happened? That I did not see those photographs? That the boy is not dead? The Soviets won't accept that, Harry. They will not accept that. And neither will I. It is a diplomatic impossibility.

HARRY: You want me to confess to something that I did not do. I did not betray my oath of office.

MICHAEL: (*Ignoring him.*) If you confess, you could then be retired . . .

HARRY: No. I cannot do that.

MICHAEL: That way, we get what we want, Harry. *Silence.*

HARRY: Silence. And the boy will have died for nothing.

MICHAEL: He died for nothing, anyway. He was a throwaway. Expendable. Disposable. But the boy's death is not the problem! You are the problem! You hid this from me, Harry. You hid your weakness—your susceptibility. God knows what else is hidden in there, waiting to bring you down.

HARRY: (*Pause.*) And you with me. Yes? (*Pause.*) You're cutting me loose, aren't you. You're cutting me loose and walking away—because you can't afford to know me. You can't afford the fact that I was your friend. That you put your trust in me—that you sent me to Moscow. It doesn't matter—does it—that I did not betray your trust. That I was loyal to my posting and my country.

That couldn't matter less. All that matters is that you are standing there, poised on the brink of becoming Prime Minister—and I am here, hanging around your neck.

MICHAEL: The country, Harry. The country.

HARRY: Like hell, the country. This is all about you.

MICHAEL: (*Ignoring this.*) You have a choice to make. A murder trial— or the confession of a misdemeanour— and retirement, abroad. Surely the choice is obvious. I know what I would do. And I'm trusting you'll do the same.

HARRY: (*Quietly.*) You may know what you would do— but you don't have to do it. *I* have to do it. And I won't. To be loyal, I must appear to be disloyal—to the end of my days. Throw over everything I've stood for, all my life. No. No, Mike. No. I'd rather die. (*Pause.*) Mike. Say something. Please.

MICHAEL: (*Long pause.*) I think nothing more need be said.

(JACKMAN *enters the sunroom.*)

Shall I hear from you—before the day is out?

HARRY: Yes. (*Beat.*) Yes.

MICHAEL: Good-bye, then.

HARRY: Yes. Indeed. Good-bye.

(MICHAEL *makes for the sunroom, where he confers with*
JACKMAN.)

SCENE SIXTEEN

(DIANA *and* MARIAN *enter.* DIANA *carries red maple
leaves.*)

DIANA: Oh—I had no idea. It's so beautiful down there.
The leaves! I haven't picked leaves like this since I was
a child.

MARIAN: Look, Harry. I found stones. (*She holds out her
hand.*) Three round, perfect stones.

(MAHAVOLITCH *enters the sunroom, dressed as in Act
One, with shirt and tie.* MICHAEL *turns his back on*
MAHAVOLITCH *and finishes his talk with* JACKMAN.)

DIANA: Someone's visiting.

HARRY: Yes.

(MICHAEL *is preparing to exit—final handshakes with*
JACKMAN *and* MAHAVOLITCH.)

DIANA: Looks like Michael.

HARRY: It is.

(MARIAN *moves away—avoiding the sunroom.*
MICHAEL *exits along the walkway—not looking back.*)

DIANA: Don't people say good-bye any more?

HARRY: Not always.

DIANA: I'm going to put these in a vase.

(DIANA *exits through the sunroom.* MARIAN *looks at her find.*)

MARIAN: Three round, perfect stones, Harry. One for each of us. Oh . . .

(HARRY *watches her sadly. He crosses and takes the umbrella, which he closes.*
MUSIC: *Japanese flute song.*
LIGHTS *brighten—almost pure white.* MARIAN *shades her eyes.*)

HARRY: What is it?

MARIAN: Make the spinning *stop*, Harry. Make it stop.

HARRY: It's all right. It's all right.

MARIAN: I want—I just want to be still.

(HARRY *leads her to the bench, where she sits.* LIGHTS *alter.*)

SCENE SEVENTEEN

(*Sunroom.* JACKMAN *and* MAHAVOLITCH *are returning files to folders.* DIANA *enters with leaves in a vase. She carries them to where the flowers already sit.*)

DIANA: There. Yes?

JACKMAN: Beautiful.

DIANA: Yes.

(DIANA *begins to remove dead flowers from the vase.* MAHAVOLITCH *goes upstage to work with papers— turning his back.*)

When we met, you said you knew all about me. Everything. Down there—walking with my mother, I was thinking about your having said that. And what I knew about myself before all this began. And what I know now. And what I don't know. And it occurred to me that, one day, it might be interesting if you were to examine others in the light of what you know about

yourself. That's what I intend to do. At least—I'm
going to try. I just thought I'd say so.

(*She takes the dead flowers and exits. Sunroom* LIGHTS
begin to fade.)

JACKMAN: Interesting woman.

MAHAVOLITCH: (*Smiling.*) Yeah.

JACKMAN: Dangerous.

(LIGHTS *fade completely.*)

SCENE EIGHTEEN

(*The garden.* MARIAN *is seated on the bench*—DIANA *is
on the sunroom steps*—HARRY *slowly paces to one side.*
JACKMAN *and* MAHAVOLITCH *are in the sunroom,
filing papers.*)

MARIAN: Where are we now, Harry? A garden somewhere. I love it here. In any garden anywhere, I feel as if
I can breathe again . . . and the sun. Here we are—at the
top of a hill. There's a river down there. We've been
here before, I know we have—but I don't know when.
Not that it matters. *When* doesn't matter any more.

Where doesn't matter. (*Beat.*) I want . . . something.
Something is missing. What can it be? Are you there?

HARRY: Yes.

MARIAN: How old are we, Harry, now?

HARRY: I don't remember.

MARIAN: Nagasaki . . . Athens . . . Cairo . . .

HARRY: (*Finishing litany.*) Moscow. Yes.

(HARRY *crosses down and puts his hand on her shoulder.*)

MARIAN: Is that you?

HARRY: Yes. Is that you?

MARIAN: Yes.

(HARRY *kisses the top of her head. The dog barks in the
ravine.*)

We're alive, Harry.

HARRY: Yes. We're alive.

(MARIAN *arranges her stones on the bench in the sun.*
MAHAVOLITCH *exits.*)

MARIAN: Do you forgive me?

HARRY: Why? What for?

MARIAN: Something I did. I don't know . . . Mischa. Is that right?

HARRY: Not to worry. It's over, now. Done with. (*Beat.*) I love you, Marian.

(DIANA *looks at her parents.*)

What a long time it's been. What a long life we've had—together and apart. Alone and together. Before there was you—before that, I . . . (*He stops—begins again.*) All my life, I've been a diplomat. Born in a pinstripe suit. First word I said was "no." Carefully. Carefully. Stood with my arms at my sides. Always at *attention.* Look at me right now, Diana. Yes? Must have been the very first view you had of your father: *man at attention.* Pinstripes. Waiting . . . Standing at attention, waiting for someone else—always someone else—to make the first move. Even you, Diana. "Are you my father?" (*He smiles.*) Yes. I am. Yes—I am.

MARIAN: (*Not moving.*) I love you, Harry.

HARRY: Yes. You love me. (*Beat.*) Yes. You love me. (*Beat.*) What a piece of news that was, the first time I heard it! *Marian loves me* . . . (*Beat.*) Not like the first news I had.

The very first news I received was that my parents had died. I was six years old. Six. "There's been an accident," someone said. "There's been . . . a terrible accident." (*Beat.*) And my guardian—my uncle said to me: "I will show you how to survive." Stand up straight—stare life in the face—and tell it you have come to bargain for terms. When it says "I want you—just as you are"—tell it "No—not without terms." Negotiate. Diplomacy. Restraint. But I was . . . I was I. Me: hidden. What you have to learn, I discovered, is how to hide out in the open. That was the bargain. Those were the terms. *Don't.* Then I fell in love—a long, long time ago—with Francis Oliver. That was when I made my choice. To live incognito. And so, we never embraced. We never touched. I never held him—never. Francis knew, of course—knew that I loved him. I'll never know if he loved me. But he said to me: "You are my stillborn lover, Harry." True. Yes. True. And he went to Spain and died. Leaving me with everything unsaid. Until I met you.

MARIAN: I love you, Harry.

HARRY: Yes. And I—dear God, how I love you. But I have been your stillborn lover, too, passing through your life on a diplomatic passport . . .

MARIAN: What is it, Harry? What's the matter? Why are you crying?

HARRY: I'm not. I never cry. (*Pause.*) I hope you heard what I said. I hope you can hear me.

MARIAN: Yes. I can hear you.

HARRY: I want to tell you something, Marian.

MARIAN: Yes.

HARRY: Diana, would you be good enough to get your mother and me a drink?

DIANA: Of course.

(DIANA *goes to the sunroom drinks table.*)

HARRY: For our life together—for our lives—I thank you.

MARIAN: Yes. (*Pause.*) The dog has stopped barking, Harry.

HARRY: Yes. It has.

MARIAN: (*Pause.*) Harry?

HARRY: Yes?

MARIAN: Are we saying good-bye?

HARRY: (*Pause.*) Yes.

MARIAN: I'm afraid. Are you?

HARRY: A little.

MARIAN: May we sit—for just a moment?

HARRY: Of course.

(*He sits beside her.* MARIAN *hands him one of the stones.*)

MARIAN: Here. It's your move.

(*The* LIGHTS *alter to isolate them.*)

Coda

(DIANA *and* JACKMAN *remain in place.* MICHAEL,
JULIET, *and* MAHAVOLITCH *enter onto the
walkways.*)

MARIAN: (*Voice over.*) When the game of Go is over, the
one who loses must approach the Master of Go and ask
him: "Where did I go wrong?" The Master always
replies with the same answer: "Where did you go
wrong? Everywhere."

(*They all freeze.*
MUSIC: *Three final chords.*
LIGHTS *dim. The play ends.*)